Emotion Recognition - Recent Advances, New Perspectives and Applications

Edited by Seyyed Abed Hosseini

Published in London, United Kingdom

Emotion Recognition - Recent Advances, New Perspectives and Applications
http://dx.doi.org/10.5772/intechopen.104074
Edited by Seyyed Abed Hosseini

Contributors
Soo-Koung Jun, Sook Hee Ryue, Uma Maheswari Pandyan, Mohamed Mansoor Roomi Sindha, Priya Kannapiran, Senthilarasi Marimuthu, Vinora Anbunathan, Michele Mukeshimana, Abraham Niyongere, Jérémie Ndikumagenge, Martins E. Irhebhude, Adeola O. Kolawole, Goshit Nenbunmwa Amos, Udo Wagner, Klaus Dürrschmid, Sandra Pauser, Alexander I. Iliev, Neha Garg, Kamlesh Sharma

First published in London, United Kingdom, 2023 by IntechOpen
IntechOpen is the global imprint of INTECHOPEN LIMITED, registered in England and Wales, registration number: 11086078, 5 Princes Gate Court, London, SW7 2QJ, United Kingdom

British Library Cataloguing-in-Publication Data
A catalogue record for this book is available from the British Library

Additional hard and PDF copies can be obtained from orders@intechopen.com

Emotion Recognition - Recent Advances, New Perspectives and Applications
Edited by Seyyed Abed Hosseini
p. cm.
Print ISBN 978-1-83768-577-6
Online ISBN 978-1-83768-578-3
eBook (PDF) ISBN 978-1-83768-579-0

Meet the editor

Seyyed Abed Hosseini received his BSc and MSc in Electrical Engineering and Biomedical Engineering in 2006 and 2009, respectively. He received his Ph.D. in Electrical Engineering from Ferdowsi University of Mashhad, Iran, in 2016. He is currently an assistant professor at the Department of Electrical Engineering, Mashhad Branch, Islamic Azad University, Mashhad, Iran. He has a multidisciplinary background and 15 years of teaching experience. He has published more than eighty peer-reviewed papers and book chapters. His research interests include cognitive science, signal processing, image processing, biological modeling, control systems, and artificial intelligence.

Contents

Preface

The brain, as the most complex organ of the body, has long been the focus of many researchers. Researching cognitive aspects of brain activity, such as emotion, helps us to understand how the brain works in different situations.

Recognizing human emotions is an important field of affective computing. Emotion is a very complex phenomenon and varies from person to person. The complex nature of emotions makes the cognitive process challenging. Emotion affects many cognitive processes, such as perception, decision-making, creativity, learning, memory, and attention. Different emotional states of a person can be inferred through external and internal reactions that change in different situations. Emotion recognition has become a research milestone in many fields, including cognitive science, neuroscience, computer science, psychology, and artificial intelligence [1].

What are emotions? Researchers have not yet been able to reach an agreement on the best definition of emotion. First, emotional phenomena are diverse. For example, some of the things we call "emotions", such as fear, seem to be associated with certain emotional experiences, while others seem to be a state we experience at a particular time or period. Second, emotions are usually divided into types such as fear, anger, joy, sadness, or pride, to name just a few. The problem is that we cannot assume that what is true of one type of emotion is true of others. Third, emotional episodes are complex. Typical emotional cycles include sensory perceptions, physiological changes, conscious emotions, cognitive processes, motivational components, and, according to many, some form of evaluation. So, what are emotions, or what are their main components, and how do the different parts relate to each other? [2].

Emotions are usually investigated in the two-dimensional space of valence arousal. In the two-dimensional model, the valence axis ranges from negative to positive and the arousal axis ranges from low to high stimulation. In emotional states, there is a rewarding and punishing behavior, for example, when a person experiences a positive emotion, they engage in behaviors that cause it to be reproduced, and when they experience a negative emotion, they avoid behaviors that cause it to reoccur.

Emotion recognition research mainly uses non-physiological signals such as facial expression, speech, and body movement, as well as physiological signals and images such as electrical skin resistance (GSR), heart rate (HR), electrocardiogram (ECG), functional magnetic resonance imaging (fMRI), electroencephalogram (EEG) and magnetoencephalogram (MEG) [3–10]. Recognizing different emotional states can also be obtained from facial images, but sometimes this method does not lead to the desired results. Compared to non-physiological signals, physiological signals are not influenced by the external environment and volition; therefore, physiological signals and especially EEG signals are more suitable for estimating the state of emotions. This book discusses the evaluation of emotions using different methods and examines recent developments, perspectives, and applications in the field.

Seyyed Abed Hosseini
Department of Electrical Engineering,
Mashhad Branch,
Islamic Azad University,
Mashhad, Iran

References

[1] Hosseini SA. Classification of brain activity in emotional states using HOS analysis. International Journal of Image, Graphics and Signal Processing. 2012;**4**(1):21

[2] Tappolet C. Emotions, Values, and Agency. Oxford University Press; 2016

[3] Hosseini SA, Khalilzadeh MA, Homam SM, Azarnoosh M. Emotional stress detection using nonlinear and higher order spectra features in EEG signal. Journal of Electrical Engineering. 2010;**39**(2)

[4] Hosseini SA, Khalilzadeh MA, Naghibi-Sistani MB, Homam SM. Emotional stress recognition using a new fusion link between electroencephalogram and peripheral signals. Iranian Journal of Neurology. 2015;**14**(3):142

[5] Hosseini SA, Khalilzadeh MA. Emotional stress recognition system using EEG and psychophysiological signals: Using new labelling process of EEG signals in emotional stress state. In: 2010 International Conference on Biomedical Engineering and Computer Science (ICBECS). IEEE; 2010. pp. 1-6

[6] Hosseini SA, Naghibi-Sistani MB. Classification of Emotional Stress Using Brain Activity [Internet]. INTECH Open Access Publisher; 2011

[7] Hosseini SA, Khalilzadeh MA. Emotional stress recognition system for affective computing based on bio-signals. Journal of Biological Systems. 2010;**18**(spec01):101-114

[8] Khalilzadeh MA, Homam SM, Hosseini SA, Niazmand V. Qualitative and quantitative evaluation of brain activity in emotional stress. Iranian Journal of Neurology. 2010;**8**(28):605-618

[9] Hosseini SA, Khalilzadeh MA, Naghibi-Sistani MB, Niazmand V. Higher order spectra analysis of EEG signals in emotional stress states. In: 2010 Second International Conference on Information Technology and Computer Science (ITCS). IEEE; 2010. pp. 60-63

[10] Hosseini SA, Khalilzadeh MA, Homam SM, Azarnoosh M. Presenting a cognitive map and computational model of the brain activity in emotional stress state. Journal of Advances in Cognitive Science. 2010;**12**(1):1-16

Chapter 1

Perspective on Dark-Skinned Emotion Recognition Using Deep-Learned and Handcrafted Feature Techniques

Martins E. Irhebhude, Adeola O. Kolawole and Goshit Nenbunmwa Amos

Abstract

Image recognition has been widely used in various fields of applications such as human—computer interaction, where it can enhance fluency, accuracy, and naturalness in interaction. The need to automate the decision on human expression is high. This paper presents a technique for emotion recognition and classification based on a combination of deep-learned and handcrafted features. Residual Network (ResNet) and Rotation Invariant Local Binary Pattern (RILBP) features were combined and used as features for classification. The aim is to classify, identify, and make judgment on facial images from dark-skinned facial images. Facial Expression Recognition 2013 (FER2013) and self-captured dark-skinned datasets were used for the experiment and validated. The result showed 93.4% accuracy on FER dataset and 95.5% on self-captured dataset, which proved the efficiency of the proposed model.

Keywords: emotion recognition, facial expression, ResNet learned features, facial emotion, self-constructed features

1. Introduction

The comprehension of pictures and classification is a very simple job for humans but a costly task in the case of computers [1]. Computer vision gives the computer similar capability to understand information from images as the human brain [2]. Identifying and classifying human facial expression is a challenging and interesting research area; it involves understanding the facial features and their behaviors. A number of facial characteristics must be retrieved from the expression of a certain individual in order to perform expression recognition. Emotion recognition has been widely used in several fields of applications like security surveillance, teaching, and neuromarketing. Classifying facial features into one of the many different categories of emotion is necessary for emotion recognition [3].

Emotion is a state of mind that includes multiple behaviors, acts, thoughts, and feelings; throughout communication, emotion plays a central role [4]. According to Pal and Sudeep [5], emotion recognition is the process of identifying human emotion, most typically from facial expressions. The different types of expressions namely joy, sadness, surprise, angers human emotions are spontaneous, consciously felt mental states that are accompanied by physical changes in the muscles of the face that suggest facial expression. Happy, sad, angry, disgusted, fearful, surprised, and neutral emotions are only a few crucial facial expressions that are used to recognize emotion [3].

The term Deep Neural Network (DNN) or Deep Learning (DL) refers to multi-layered Artificial Neural Network (ANN). This has been considered one of the most discussed Artificial Intelligence (AI) techniques in image classification in the last few decades, with strong instruments, and is very common in the literature as it has a large amount of data to manage. DL achieved its successes over the classical machine learning models because of the multiple deeper layers [6]. There are several DL models that are trained using large labeled datasets and neural network architectures that learn features automatically from the data without using manual feature extraction.

Recent technological advances have led to the use of the Artificial Intelligence System, as these systems are capable of understanding and realizing emotion recognition through facial features. This is also an attempt to prove the existence of the latest technical advances for human-computer interaction using Deep Learning or Convolution Neural Network (CNN) models [7]. Recently, Deep Learning has become a vital tool for numerous applications; they are made up of various processing layers for data representations with various degrees of abstraction. These layers are composed of simple but non-linear modules, each transforming the representation at one level (starting with the raw input) into a representation at a higher, slightly more abstract level [8]. Deep-learning techniques perform well in tackling a wide range of computer vision issues that cannot be solved by conventional machine-learning methods. The accuracy of deep-learning applications has surpassed that of traditional applications in a number of computer-vision tasks, along with breaking previous records for tasks like image recognition [9]. Though deeper neural networks are more difficult to train, He and Zhang [10] offered a Residual learning framework (ResNet) to make it simpler to train networks that are much deeper than those previously employed. Instead of learning unreferenced functions, the study deliberately reformulated the layers to learn residual functions with reference to the layer inputs. Zhang offered in-depth empirical proof that these residual networks are simpler to optimize and can improve accuracy over considerably increased depth. The current popular CNN algorithm, combined with the ResNet-50 residual network, has achieved a good effect in the multi-classification tasks [11].

Image recognition, most especially the need to automate the decision on human expression, is on the high need, bearing in mind that determining the features to extract is next to impossible because of the variance in the facial features of different races and gender and individual specific differences like accident victims or those disfigured from birth [12].

In this research, image classification is carried out using a combination of deep-learned and handcrafted features for classification of facial expressions. A Rotation Invariant Local Binary Pattern (RILBP) and a pre-trained ResNet representation of images are employed for feature extraction from the set of data, which have been proven to increase accuracy in training deeper neural networks by eliminating the problem of degradation and vanishing/exploding gradient, which has been largely addressed by introducing a deep residual network and normalized initialization.

The limited work done with images of some races, the Negroid specifically, leads to little or no dataset of such in recent time, which, in turn, affects the accuracy of results if tested with this race [13]. Hence, automating this process would go a long way in balancing the request and service, and also, allowing the dataset to be trained by deep-learning algorithm is most likely the optimized solution in solving this problem. This study will also generate dataset that will help handle dark-race emotion classification.

The remainder of this paper is organized as follows: Section 2 provides the background of the study; Section 3 reviews the related works. The proposed method is introduced and detailed in Section 4. The experiments and results are illustrated in Section 4. Finally, Section 5 provides the conclusion and some perspectives for future researches.

2. Background of the study

Residual Network and Rotation Invariant Local Binary Pattern background subjects will be discussed in this section.

2.1 Residual networks architecture

The accuracy of the CNN-based emotion classification system has been improved through pre- or post-processing and the development of new algorithms and models in the architecture. Szegedy and Liu [14] reveal that network depth (stacking more layers) is of great importance, but this comes with a problem of vanishing/exploding gradients, which hamper convergence from the beginning. Normalized initialization and immediate normalization layer solve these problems [15].

In deep-learning models, more layers are added to learn more complex problems, but this addition leads to degradation of the performance and saturated accuracy; the degradation does not cause overfitting [16], When a network overfits, training error decreases, while test errors increase; with degradation, higher training error is reported as deeper networks are difficult to train [17].

He and Zhang [10] introduced the deep ResNet learning framework made from residual blocks to address these problems. The core idea of the residual block is the skip connection in which there is a connection that skips one or more layers. Skipping effectively simplifies the network by using fewer networks in the initial training stage. ResNet has different architectures in which their difference is in the number of layers such as ResNet-34, which uses 34 layers; ResNet-152 with 152 layers; and ResNet-18 with 18 layers. These are plain network architectures inspired by VGG-19 in which the shortcut connection is added [16]. ResNet is made up of convolutional layers, residual blocks, and fully connected layers. It has the concept of residual learning in which the subtraction of a feature is learned from the input of that layer by using shortcut connections. It has proven that the residual learning can improve the performance of model training and also revolve the problem of degrading accuracy in deep network [18].

ResNet makes it simpler to train networks that are much deeper than those previously employed. Instead of learning unreferenced functions, they deliberately reformulated the layers to learn residual functions with reference to the layer inputs. They offer in-depth empirical proof that these residual networks are simpler to optimize and can improve accuracy over considerably increased depth. The current popular convolutional neural network algorithm, combined with the ResNet-50 residual network, has achieved a good effect in the multi-classification task [11].

ResNet-18 model has been used by Huang and Liu [19] in identification of different grades of aluminum scrap with improved identification efficiency and reduced equipment cost. The ResNet-18 network model trained the three different datasets using the RGB, HSV, and LBP, and the results showed that RGB was the best dataset. Authors concluded that with hyperparameter optimization of the ResNet-18 model,

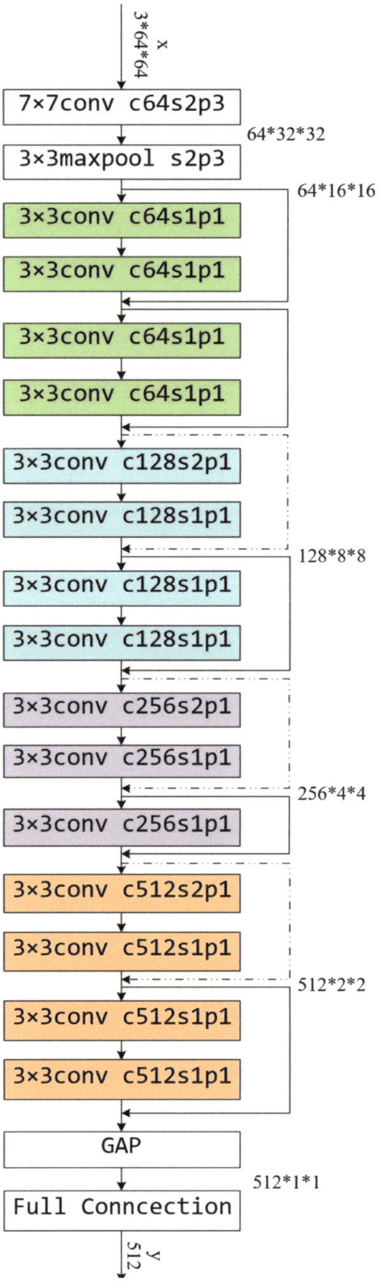

Figure 1.
Architecture of ResNet [20].

the accuracy of final classification and recognition could reach 100% and effectively achieve the classification of different grades of aluminum scrap.

Figure 1 shows image of the ResNet-18 architecture; the structure indicates an aluminum block image with an input size of 224 pixels × 224 pixels × 3 channels. In the neural network structure, conv represents the convolutional layer, which uses 3×3 filters; downsampling is performed by the convolution layer with a stride of 2.

Max pool is the maximum pooling layer, avg. pool is the average pooling layer, and FC is the fully connected layer, such that the size of the convolutional kernel is 7 × 7conv, the number of channels is 64, and the step size is 2 [19]. A total of eighteen layers exist in the architecture (17 convolutional layers, a fully connected layer, and an additional softmax layer to perform classification task). Throughout the network, residual shortcut connections are inserted between layers. There are two types of connections; the first is denoted by solid lines and is used when input and output have the same dimensions. The second type of connections, denoted by dotted lines, is used when dimensions increase. The layers are stacked to learn a residual mapping; the mapping function, denoted by $H(x)$ and depicted in Eq. (1), is fitted by a few stacked layers. The hypothesis behind residual layer is if several nonlinear layers can asymptotically estimate a challenging mapping function, then they do the same for the residual function denoted as $F(x)$ in Eq. (2) [21].

The underlying mapping is given by:

$$H(x)=F(x)+x \tag{1}$$

The residual function is given by

$$F(x)=H(x)-x \tag{2}$$

With x representing the input layer.

2.2 Rotation invariant local binary pattern (RILBP)

The RILBP is based on uniform local binary pattern (LBP) histograms. LBP descriptor is widely used in texture analysis because of its computational simplicity and robustness in illuminating changes. The LBP approach labels the image pixels by thresholding the 3×3 neighborhood of each pixel with the center value and summing the thresholded values weighted by powers of two [22]. It is the extension of LBP through the use of different neighborhood sizes. Rotation invariant texture analysis provides texture features that are invariant to the rotation angle of input texture image. These features are used to train different classifiers such as neural networks, Nearest Neighbor, and SVM [23]. Further details are as reported in [24].

3. Review of related literature

Emotion identification aims at recognizing a human's emotions; the emotion may be taken either from face or from verbal contact. Bodapati and Veeranjaneyulu [25] recognized human emotions from facial expressions using Extended Cohn-Kanade (CK+) benchmark dataset. Based on the experimental results, authors stated that the images were better portrayed by unsupervised features as compared to the handmade features. When face-detection algorithm was used, the accuracy was 86.04%, and without using the face-detection algorithm, the proposed model gave an accuracy of 81.36%.

To maximize the efficiency of the emotional recognition system, Cai and Hu [26] suggested a multimodal model of emotion recognition from speech and text. CNN and long-term short-term memory (LSTM) were combined in a form of binary channels to learn the features of acoustic emotion; textual features were captured with an effective bidirectional long short-term memory (Bi-LSTM) network. To learn and identify the fusion features, they used a deep-learning neural network (DNN). Experiments were carried out on the Interactive Emotional Dyadic Motion Capture (IEMOCAP) database yielding an overall increased accuracy of text recognition by 6.70%, and the accuracy of speech emotion recognition increased by 13.85%. Their experimental findings show that the multimodal recognition performance is higher than that of the single modal and outperforms other multimodal models reported on the test datasets with an accuracy of 71.25%.

Fei and Jiao [27] proposed real-time facial expression classification based on voting mechanism to increase recognition rates of facial expression classification in real-time; various models of neural networks were designed to learn the facial features. Experiment showed that the average recognition rates for fer2013, CK+, and JAFFE database were 74.58, 100, and 100%, respectively. Comparing the results to other models, their methods of recognition had superior performance, improved recognition, and algorithm robustness.

Ansari and Singh [28] presented the implementation of deep-learning model of CNN. The architecture was an adaptation of an image-processing CNN, programmed in Python using Keras model-level library and TensorFlow backend. For five emotions (happiness, fear, sadness, neutral, anger), the model achieved a mean accuracy of 79.33%, which was comparable with performances reported in scientific literatures.

Sujanaa and Palanivel [29] used datasets comprising of mouth images in the form of video frames to categorize emotions into happy, normal, and surprise. Histogram Oriented Gradient (HOG) and LBP were used to extract features, while the SVM and one-dimensional neural network were trained to detect these emotions, and accuracy of 97.44 and 98.51% were achieved, respectively.

Minaee and Minaei [30] proposed a deep-learning approach based on attentional convolutional network that concentrated on important sections of the face and made substantial improvements on multiple datasets, including Facial Expression Recognition 2013 (FER2013), Cohn-Kanade (known as CK+), Facial Expression Research Group Database (FERG), and Japanese Female Facial Expression (JAFFE), compared with previous models. A visualization technique was employed based on the performance of the classifier, and it was able to identify key facial regions for different emotions, showing sensitivity to different parts of the face.

Haar cascade classifier and CNN model were used by Shirisha and Buddha [31]. The study reported an accuracy of 62% from facial emotion detection on FER 2013 datasets and suggested use of transfer learning, more datasets, and different combinations in designing convolution layers.

Kalaivani and Sathyapriya [12] addressed methods for extraction and detection of mouth regions with the use Viola-Jones and image-cropping techniques for facial expression detection. The mouth area was extracted, and facial emotions were graded according to white pixel values in the face's picture. Edge-based segmentation and operation was applied to extract the mouth region features. By measuring the area of the mouth region and from the shape and size of the region, the expression was detected.

According to Kim and Saurous [32], machine-based emotion recognition is a daunting job, but it does have great potential to allow empathic human—machine communication. The authors proposed a model that incorporated features proven to be useful for emotion recognition and DNN to leverage temporal information when recognizing emotional status. A Berlin Emotion Speech Database (EMO-DB) benchmark was used for evaluation, achieving an efficiency of 88.9% recognition rate, outperforming other state-of-art algorithms.

Santhoshkumar and Kalaiselvi [33] analyzed human emotional states by predicting full-body movements using feed-forward deep CNN architecture and Block Average Intensity Value (BAIV) feature. Both models were tested on emotion-action dataset (University of YORK) with 15 forms of emotions. The experimental result showed the better recognition efficiency of the feed-forward deep CNN architecture with 90.09% accuracy compared to BAIV with 80.03% accuracy.

According to Selvapriya and Maria [34], identifying human facial expression is not a simple task due to lighting, facial occlusions, face color/shape, and other circumstances. Social emotional classifications were defined in their research by artificial neural network (ANN), deep learning, and a rich hybrid neural network (HNN). The study also focused on a state-of-the-art hybrid deep-learning approach, incorporating a CNN for individual-frame spatial features and long short-term memory (LSTM) for the temporal features of consecutive frames. Using Matlab, the analyzed methodologies were applied. The CNN model achieved greater classification accuracy compared to the rich HNN and ANN schemes. With a specific number of data, CNN, HNN, and ANN performed with an accuracy of 90, 70, and 58%, respectively. The performance assessment was shown to have specific advantages and disadvantages for each and every process among themselves.

Classification is very important to organize the data, so that it is easily available. Mohamed [35] explored four popular machine-learning and data-mining techniques used for classification such as Decision Tree, ANN, K-Nearest-Neighbor (KNN), and SVM. The study showed that each technique applied different datasets in different places; each technique had its own advantages and disadvantages, and it was discovered that it was very difficult to find a classifier that could identify all the datasets with the same accuracy. SVM reported the highest overall accuracy of all learning algorithms with 76.3%. The other approaches also performed well and could be a fair choice as they were all over 70% accurate. The learning algorithm's output was highly dependent upon the existence of the dataset. Krishna and Neelima [1] described the classification of images as a classic problem of the fields of image processing, computer vision, and machine learning. They investigated image classification using deep learning and AlexNet. Four test images were chosen from the ImageNet database and were classified correctly with 95% accuracy, and this demonstrated the efficacy of using AlexNet deep-learning-based image classification.

Luna-Jimenez and Kleinlein [36] proposed an automatic emotion-recognizer system that had a speech emotion recognizer (SER) and a facial emotion recognizer (FER). Eight emotions were classified, and they achieved 86.70% accuracy on the RAVDESS dataset using a subject-wise 5-CV evaluation.

Kaviya and Arumugaprakash [37] proposed a human group facial sentiment recognition system using a deep-learning approach. Haar filter was used to detect and extract facial features, with a CNN model developed to recognize facial expressions and classify them into five basic emotional states, namely, happy, sad, anger, surprise, and neutral; then, the predicted group emotions were fed into an audio synthesizer to get audio output. An accuracy rate of 65% was achieved for Facial Expression Recognition (FER)-2013 and 60% for custom datasets.

Babajee and Suddul [38] analyze how the CNN algorithm is used to identify human facial expressions using deep learning. Their system employed a labeled dataset of over 32,298 images with varied facial expressions for training and testing. A noise reduction facial detection subsystem with feature extraction was part of the pre-training process. Without the use of optimization techniques, an accuracy of 79.8% was recorded in recognizing each of the seven basic human emotions.

Awatramani and Hasteer [39] trained the fundamental architecture of CNN to recognize human emotions in children with Autism Special Disorder (ASD). The model was validated using a pre-existing dataset from the literature, and an accuracy of 67.50% was attained.

The Shanghai Jiao Tong University (SJTU) Emotion EEG dataset (SEED) was used with ResNet-50 and Adam optimizer; a CNN model was presented by Ahmad and Zhang [40] to simultaneously learn the features and recognize the emotions of positive, neutral, and negative states of pure electroencephalograms (EEG) signals. Negative emotion had the highest accuracy of 94.86%, while neutral and positive had 94.29 and 93.25%, respectively. An average accuracy of 94.13% was reported; this showed that the model's classification abilities were excellent and could improve emotion recognition.

Sandhu and Malhotra [41] classified human emotions into subcategories based on the hybrid CNN approach used to recognize them. In order to achieve the best accuracy and loss, the study used the FER13 dataset for emotion recognition and trained the model accordingly. Seven fundamental emotion classes were effectively recognized by the system. The suggested approach was therefore demonstrated to be successful in terms of increased accuracy with an average rate of 88.10% and minimal loss for facial emotion recognition.

Santoso and Kusuma [42] adopted the state-of-the-art models in ImageNet and modified the classification layer with Spinal Net Kabir, Abdar [43], and ProgressiveSpinalNet Chopra [44] architecture to improve the accuracy. The categorization was done using the FER2013 dataset; after the training procedure was completed and its hyperparameter adjusted, an accuracy of 74.4% was achieved. The study in [45] provided an end-to-end system that used residual blocks to identify emotions and improve accuracy in the research field. After receiving a facial image, the framework returned its emotional state. The accuracy obtained on the test set of FERGIT dataset (an extension of the FER2013 dataset with 49,300 images) was 75%.

Zhu and Fu [46] integrated CNN with VGGNet, AlexNet, and LeNet-5. They also introduced optimized Central Local Binary Pattern (CLBP) algorithm into the CNN to construct a CNN-CLBP algorithm for facial emotion recognition. The experiment yielded accuracy of 88.16% for the hybrid CNN-LBP, while LBP, LeNet-5, and VGGNet gave 48.63, 73.22, and 83.17% accuracy, respectively.

Durga and Rajesh [47] proposed a 2D-ResNet convolutional neural network to detect maskable images of facial emotions; better performance metrics were obtained in terms of accuracy of 99.3%, recall of 99.12%, F1 score of 0.98%, and sensitivity of 99.16%. The proposed model reduced the problem of overfitting.

Irhebhude and Kolawole [24] focused on presenting a technique that categorized gender among dark-skinned people. The classification was done using SVM on sets of images gathered locally and publicly. Analysis includes face detection using Viola-Jones algorithm, extraction of Histogram of Oriented Gradient and Rotation Invariant

LBP (RILBP) features, and training with SVM classifier. PCA was performed on both the HOG and the RILBP descriptors to extract high dimensional features. Various success rates were recorded; however, PCA on RILBP performed best with an accuracy of 99.6 and 99.8%, respectively, on the public and local datasets.

Irhebhude and Kolawole [48], in their study, implemented an age estimation system from facial images using the Rotation Invariant Local Binary Pattern Descriptor (RILBD) feature, which was combined with Principal Component Analysis (PCA) for feature high dimensional data, and the Support Vector Machine (SVM) algorithm was used for classification. The facial images were grouped into four classes, namely, class 1 (0–10 years), class 2 (11–20 years), class 3 (21–35 years), and class 4 (above 35 years). Experiments were carried out on the local dataset captured within Kaduna metropolis in the northern part of Nigeria and the FGNET dataset, which is publicly available online, to test the performance of the proposed method. They reported that the system achieved overall accuracy result of 95.0 and 95.7% on the two datasets. This was reported to show the impact self-constructed features could have in the overall accuracy of a recognition task.

In this work, the conventional ResNet features will be extracted and combined with RILBP features and used as a feature set to recognize seven different facial emotions.

4. Methodology

The proposed method is based on the combination of information from both the deep-learned features and RILBP, as shown in **Figure 2**. The methodology consists

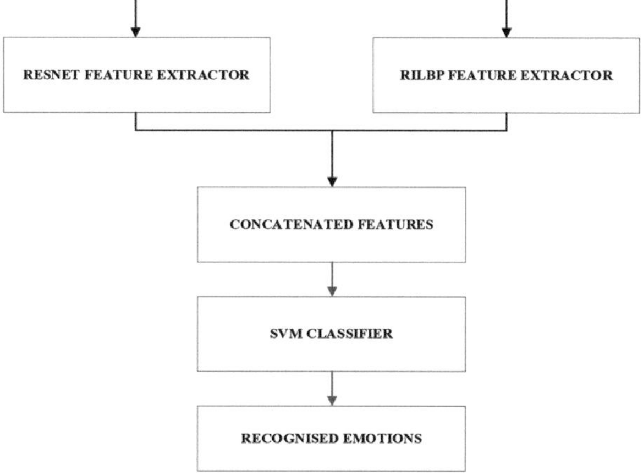

Figure 2.
Proposed methodology.

of four steps: input image, face detection/cropping, feature extraction, and feature classification.

The proposed methodology is made up of the following steps: input image, face detection & cropping, feature extraction and concatenation, and feature classification and emotion recognition as illustrated in **Figure 2**.

4.1 Input image

In this step, captured facial images with various sizes were loaded into the system for further processes to take place. The images in its original form were fed to the next stage of the methodology; these images consist of the entire face captured.

For this study, experiments were carried out on self-captured dataset and the FER2013 database [49]. The focus is to recognize and classify seven (7) different emotions from facial images using deep convolutional neural network.

The self-captured database consists of 5509 images of Black faces. The images were gotten from snapshots of different people, both male and female, with the use of a digital camera. The faces consisting of facial details and expressions were saved and used to make up the dataset. The images were of various sizes, consisting of 652 'angry' images, 778 'disgust' images, 519 'fear' images, 1168 'happy' images, 908 'neutral' images, 830 'sad' images, and 654 'surprise' images.

4.2 Face detection & cropping

The image part of the face was detected automatically, and the detected face position was cropped accordingly [50]. The Viola-Jones algorithm, as described in Irhebhude, Kolawole [24], was used for face detection. The feature works with images in squares, with multiple pixels in each box. Per box is then processed, yielding various values, indicating dark and light areas. These values serve as the basis for image processing. To improve image quality, the pictures were cropped and standardized to 224×224×3 (ResNet specifications).

Figure 3 shows sample images of each of the seven classes of emotion in the dataset: angry, disgust, fear, happy, neutral, sad, and surprised. These seven facial emotions were formed by each subject after careful examination of the FER2013 datasets. This was done so that dark-skinned faces can be adequately captured for the

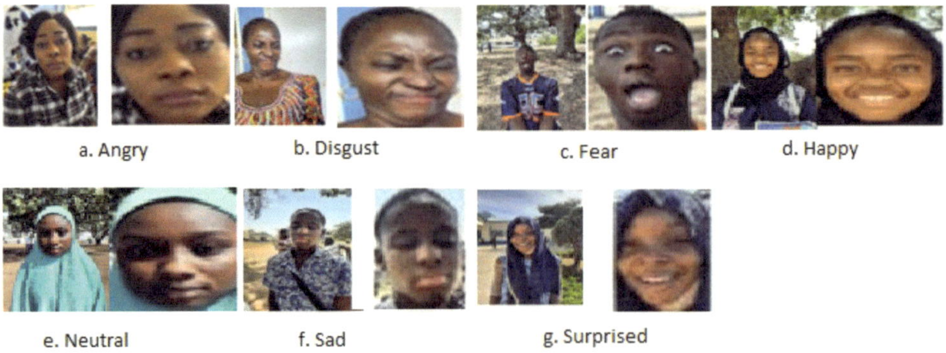

Figure 3.
Sample images of different classes of emotions before and after face detection from self-captured dataset.

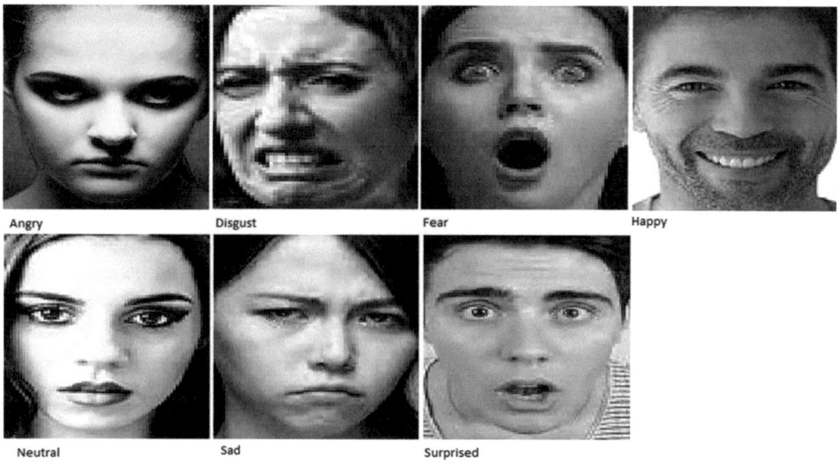

Figure 4.
Sample images of different classes of emotions from FER2013 dataset [49].

purpose of the experiment. Each class has two sample images, one in original form and the other after detection; the detected faces are used for the experiment.

The FER2013 dataset consists of grayscale images of 48x48 pixels in size. The faces have been automatically registered so that the face is centered and occupies about the same amount of space in each image. Each face is categorized based on the emotion shown in the facial expression into one of seven categories: angry, disgust, fear, happy, sad, surprise, and neutral images [49]. The training set consists of 28,709 images; the database was created using Google image search API; the FER has more variations, including occlusion, partial faces, eye glasses, and low contrast [30]. Sample images are shown in **Figure 4**.

4.3 Feature extraction

Two feature extraction algorithms, ResNet and RILBP, were used to extract facial emotion features. The ResNet features are extracted from the pooling layer of the input image, while RILBP extracts texture features that are invariant to rotation [23].

ResNet-18 was used in order to extract deep-learned features from the detected and cropped facial images; the network uses an 18-layer plain network architecture as inspired by VGG-19 in which the shortcut connection is added [16]. This network is adapted for the emotion classification task as it is suitable to extract learned image features. Optimization was done with Bayesian optimization, with features automatically extracted before the fully connected layer giving a feature length of 512.

To enhance the description ability, the RILBP descriptor was used; this encodes the local facial features in a multi-resolution spatial histogram and combines the distribution of local intensity with the spatial information [23]. Studies have shown good results for gender recognition and age estimation Irhebhude, Kolawole [24], using the RILBP descriptor. Following the steps as reported by the authors, the technique extracted texture features with a dimension length of 36 for further classification.

Concatenating the RILBP and ResNet features takes benefits from their advantages to yield a good performance. The combined/concatenated features were presented to the SVM classifier.

4.4 Feature classification: SVM classifier

The feature sets extracted are used as input in the classification stage. SVM was used for model training, because of its popularity and simplicity. Optimizable SVM was used to train the classifier to help select the best parameter for classifying facial images into the seven different emotion categories. The best hyper-plane that can separate samples of one class from those of other classes using different types of support vectors was obtained using the SVM method by Dammak, Mliki [23]; the hyperparameter optimization automatically selects the hyperparameter values for classification. This model seeks to minimize the model classification error and returns a model with the optimized hyperparameters. In the proposed method, the optimizable parameters were: the kernel function, box constraint level, multiclass method, and standardize data. The linear kernel function with box-level constraint parameter was set to 1 to prevent overfitting and multiclass method of one-vs-one;

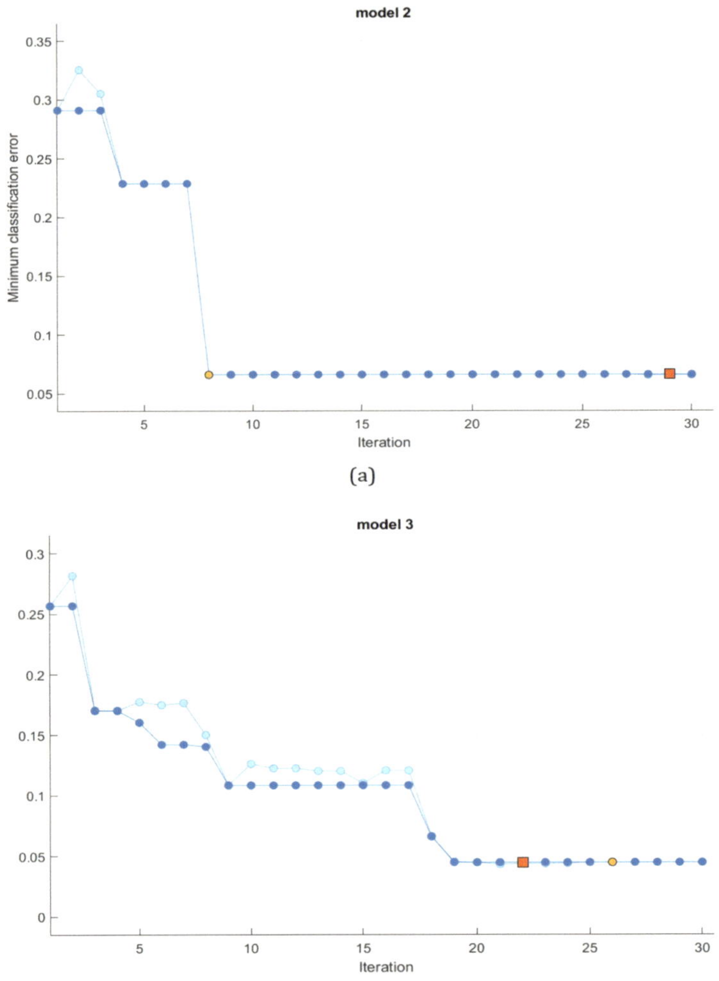

(a)

(b)

Figure 5.
Minimum classification error plot. (a) FER dataset; (b) Self-captured dataset.

model hyperparameters were set to optimize. These parameters were used in training the model, and the minimum classification error plot (**Figure 5**) shows the optimized results.

Figure 5 illustrates the minimum classification error plot. At each iteration, a different combination of hyperparameter value is tried and updated on the plot with the minimum validation classification error observed up to that iteration; this is indicated in dark blue. On completion of the optimization process, a set of optimized hyperparameters is selected, which is indicated by a red square.

The red square indicates the iteration that corresponds to the optimized hyperparameters. The yellow point indicates the iteration that corresponds to the hyperparameters that yield the observed minimum classification error.

5. Experimental result

To evaluate performance of the proposed technique, 70% of the data was used for training, while 30% was used as test data. The test results were visualized and explained using confusion matrix, scatter plot, and ROC curve.

Experiments were conducted to validate the use of concatenating ResNet and RILBP as feature extractors on each of the datasets. Optimizable SVM was used and hyperparameters were automatically as kernel function: linear, box constraint:1, multiclass method: one-vs-one and standardize data set as true. An accuracy of 93.4% was

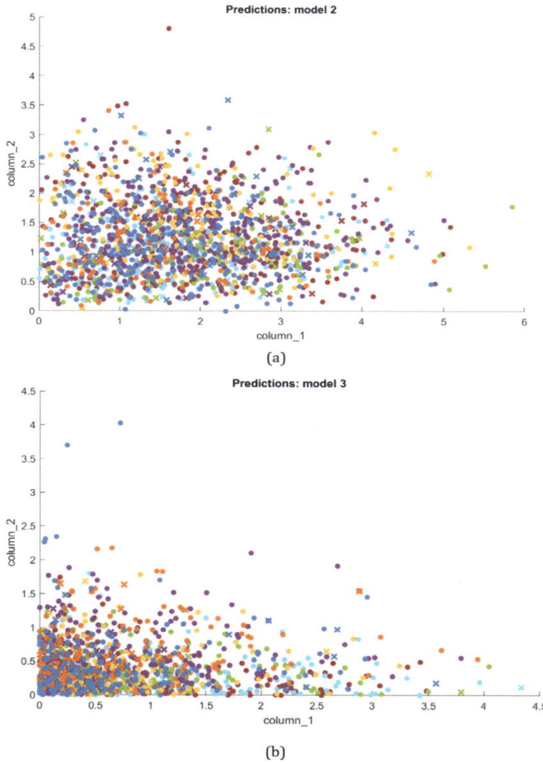

Figure 6.
Scatter plot visualization of sample images. (a) FER dataset; (b) Self-captured dataset.

obtained on the FER dataset and 95.5% on the self-captured dataset; this indicates the percentage of correctly classified observations.

The scatter plot in **Figure 6** gives a visual representation of the scatter plot obtained; the plot uses different colors to represent the classes of emotions.

The scatter plot in **Figure 6** helps to visualize the training data and misclassified points for emotion detection on FER dataset (**Figure 6a**) and self-captured dataset (**Figure 6b**). Each colored dot represents the plot, which shows a strong relationship between the variables as the data points cluster more tightly. We also see the values tending to rise together, indicating a positive correlation; few outliers are also observed from the plot. The results show a similar pattern in the two datasets. The x indicates the misclassified instances.

The confusion matrix and ROC curve are used to check the performance of the classifier in each class. **Figure 7** displays the confusion matrix, showing the number of observations in each cell. The matrix is plotted as the true class against the predicted class; the row represents the true class, and the columns correspond to the predicted class.

The classes labeled as 1 to 7; angry is represented by class 1, while disgust, fear, happy, neutral, sad, and surprise are represented by classes 2,3,4,5,6, and

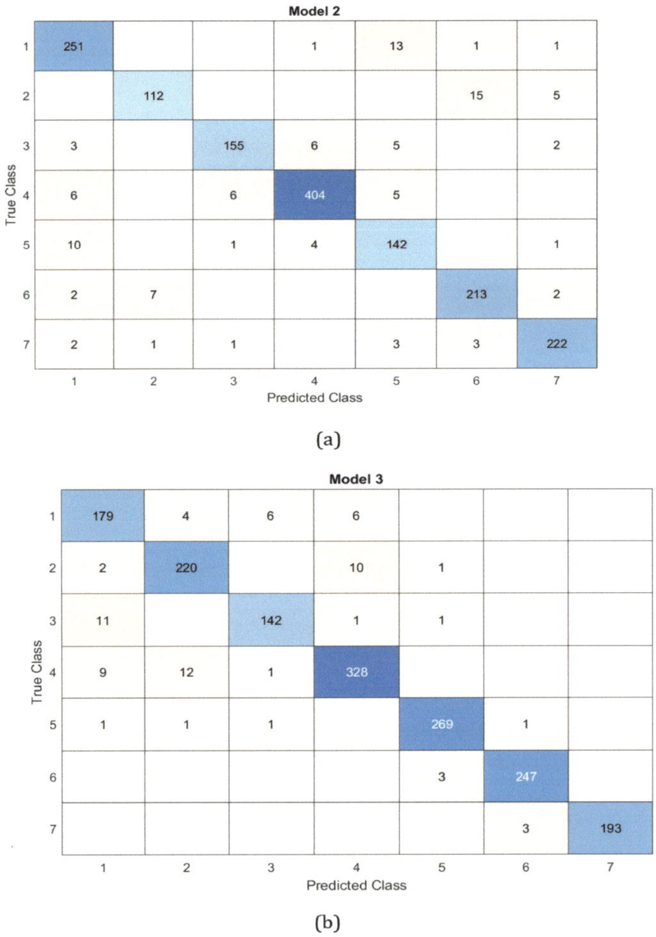

Figure 7.
Confusion matrix showing number of observations. (a) FER 2013 (b) Self-captured dataset.

7, respectively. The blue diagonal boxes show observations with the correctly predicted class; the off-diagonal cells correspond to the incorrectly classified observations. We can see for the FER dataset (**Figure 7a**) that class 7 has the least classification error rate, having 222 correct observations as class 7 and total of 10 observations wrongly placed when compared to the other classes. Similarly, from the self-captured data (**Figure 7b**), classes 6 and 7 had the least error rate, reporting 3 wrong observations each.

Figure 8 illustrates confusion matrix performance of the classifier per class, indicating the True Positive Rate (TPR) and False Negative Rate (FNR). The TPR is the proportion of correctly classified observations per true class. The FNR is the proportion of incorrectly classified observations per true class. From **Figure 8(a)**, class 2 has the highest FNR of incorrectly classified points as 15.2%, which is shown in the FNR column. Class 4 has the highest TPR value of 96.0% correctly classified points in this class. For the self-captured set in **Figure 8(b)**, class 6 recorded the least FNR and highest TPR values of 1.2 and 98.8%, respectively.

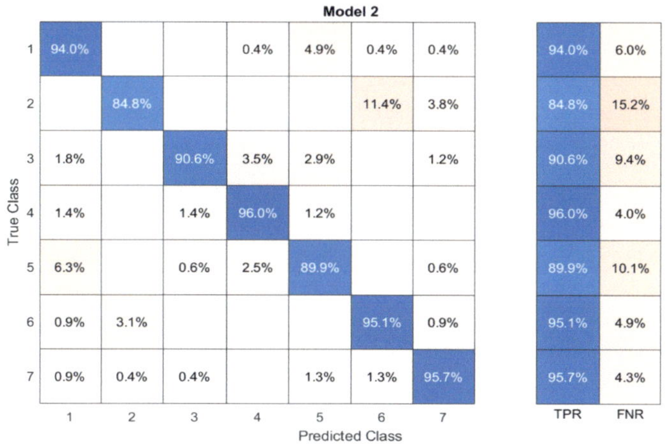

(a)

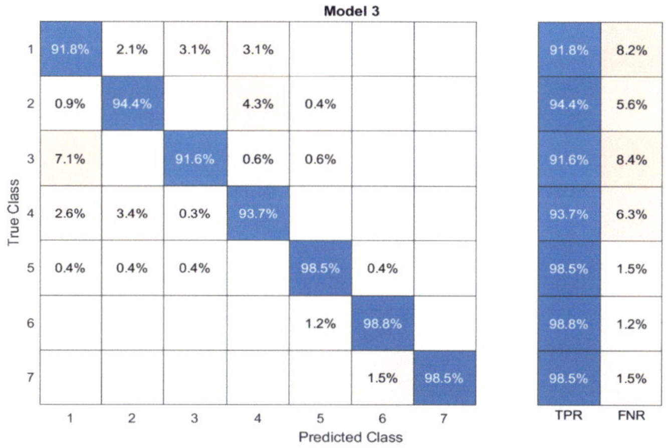

(b)

Figure 8.
Confusion matrix showing true positive rate and false negative rate. (a) FER 2013 (b) Self-captured dataset.

Figure 9 shows confusion matrix performance per predictive values to investigate the False Discovery Rate (FDR). The Positive Predictive Value (PPV) is the proportion of correctly classified observations per predicted class. The FDR is the proportion of incorrectly classified observations per predicted class. PPV is indicated in blue for the correctly predicted points in each class, and the FDR is shown in orange for the incorrectly predicted points in each class. The class 5 had the highest FDR of 15.5% incorrectly predicted class for the FER dataset, while class 1 had the highest FDR of 11.4% for the self-captured dataset, as shown in **Figure 9**.

The ROC curve in **Figure 10** shows the plot of TPR and FPR for classification scores computed by the classifier. For the FER dataset, TPR and FPR of 0.02 and 0.94, respectively, showed that 2% observations were incorrectly classified to other classes, while 94% were correctly classified to their classes. The self-captured dataset recorded a similar pattern with TPR and FPR values of 0.02 and 0.92, respectively. The overall performance is indicated with an Area Under Curve (AUC) value of 0.99 for the two

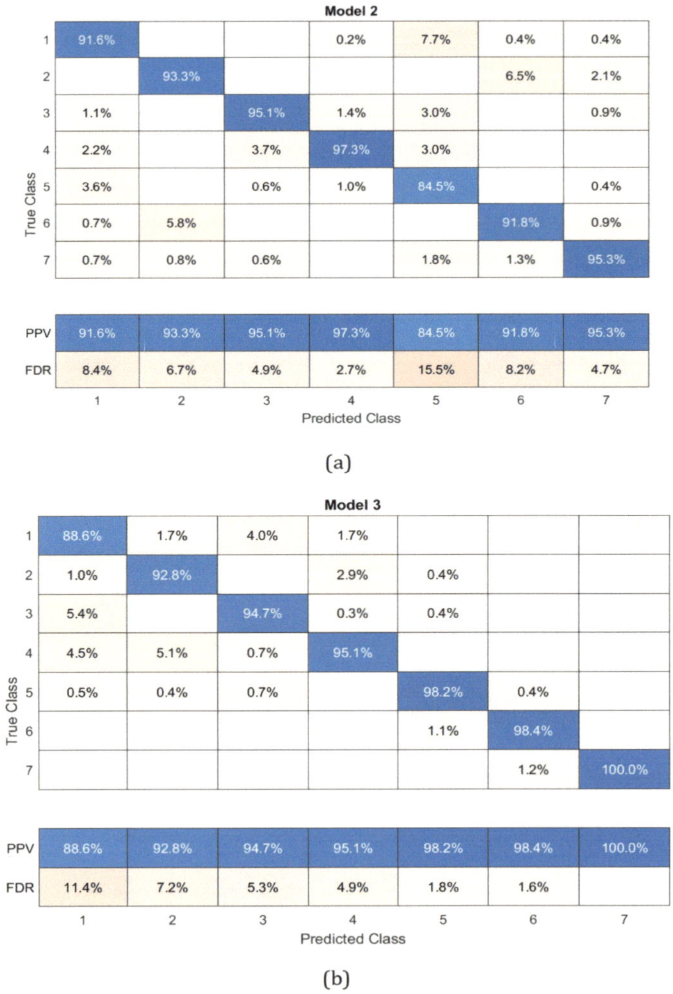

Figure 9.
Confusion matrix of positive predictive values and false discovery rates recognition. (a) FER dataset (b) Self-captured dataset.

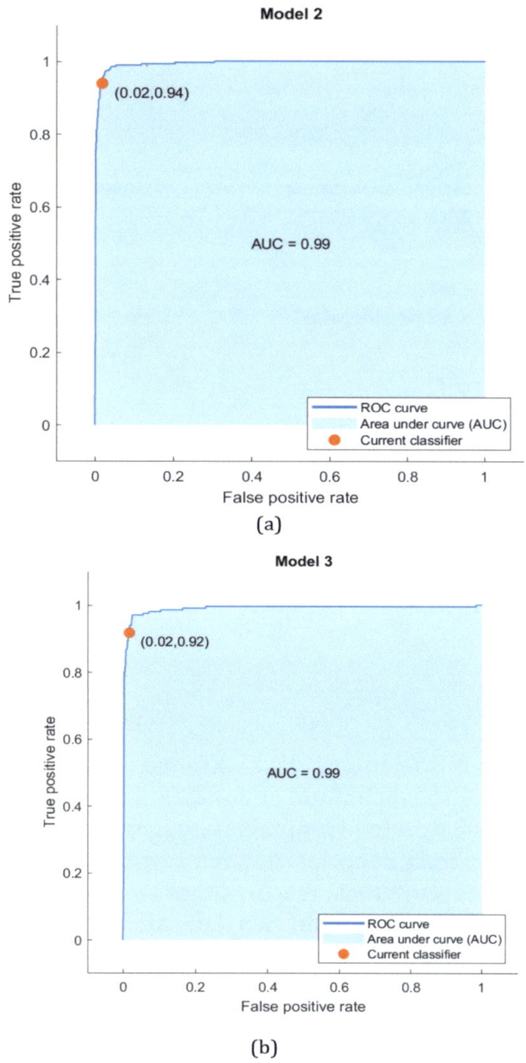

Figure 10.
ROC curve showing the classifier performance. (a) FER dataset; (b) Self-captured dataset.

datasets. This shows that the classifier has 99% overall performance; AUC values are in the range of 0 to 1, and larger values indicate better performance of classifier.

6. Comparison with selected state-of-the-art methods

The proposed technique used in this study showed a more promising result when compared with other selected methods, as presented in **Table 1**.

With a fusion of handcrafted and deep-learned features, [46] reported 88.61% accuracy, indicating that the proposed technique performed better with 5% improvement in accuracy. Referring to datasets and ResNet methods used, the proposed method achieved a gain of 10% when compared to the study in [27], which used voting technique on the FER dataset. From the experimental results, the study concludes

Author	Method	Accuracy	Dataset
Zhu et al. [46]	CNN-CLBP	88.61%	CK+ and JAFFE
	LBP	73.22%	
	VGGNET	83.17%	
Fei et al. [27]	VGG19, ResNet18 and DNN + SVM (VOTE)	74.58%	FER 2013
		100%	CK + JAFFE
		100%	
Proposed method	RILBP + ResNet18	93.3%	FERET
		95.5%	Self-Captured

Table 1.
Comparison with other methods.

that the proposed method provides a more promising result in terms of accuracy on recognition. This was a result of the combination of more transfer learning and rotation invariant features. The approach showed considerable improvements when compared with existing methods in [27, 46].

7. Conclusion

Facial emotion recognition among dark-skinned people has been addressed in this paper by adopting the technique of concatenating handcrafted and deep-learned ResNet features extracted from facial images. The ResNet transfer learning model was used to extract deep-learned features and combined with RILBP features, which helped capture local features that were invariant to scale and rotation. The method was evaluated on two datasets: self-captured (which comprised of dark-skinned facial images) and FER2013 datasets (which formed the base dataset to validate the technique). The SVM classifier was used for classification into various emotion categories. The study showed that ResNet and RILBP complement each other in terms of achieving a good recognition accuracy. Future work will look into data balancing and generating more datasets, especially of dark-skinned people.

Acknowledgements

Authors will like to appreciate the management of Nigerian Defense Academy for the support and encouragement throughout the period of this study.

Conflict of interest

The authors declare no conflict of interest.

Author details

Martins E. Irhebhude*, Adeola O. Kolawole and Goshit Nenbunmwa Amos
Department of Computer Science, Nigerian Defense Academy, Nigeria

*Address all correspondence to: mirhebhude@nda.edu.ng

References

[1] Krishna M et al. Image classification using deep learning. International Journal of Engineering & Technology. 2018;**7**(2):614-617

[2] Patil MP, Chokkalingam S. Deep convolutional neural networks (CNN) for medical image analysis. International Journal of Engineering and Advanced Technology (IJEAT). 2019;**8**(3S):607-610

[3] Verma N, Tiwari S. A review on facial expression recognition system using deep learning. Journal of Emerging Technologies and Innovative Research (JETIR). 2021;**8**(7):963-968

[4] Ruiz-Garcia A et al. Deep learning for emotion recognition in faces. In: The 25th International Conference on Artificial Neural Networks (ICANN 2016). Barcelona, Spain: Springer Verlag; 2016

[5] Pal KK, Sudeep K. Preprocessing for image classification by convolutional neural networks. In: 2016 IEEE International Conference on Recent Trends in Electronics, Information & Communication Technology (RTEICT). Bangalore, India: IEEE; 2016

[6] Albawi S, Mohammed TA, Al-Zawi S. Understanding of a convolutional neural network. In: 2017 International Conference on Engineering and Technology (ICET). Antalya, Turkey: IEEE; 2017

[7] Mohammadi F, Abadeh MS. Image steganalysis using a bee colony based feature selection algorithm. Engineering Applications of Artificial Intelligence. 2014;**31**:35-43

[8] LeCun Y, Bengio Y, Hinton G. Deep learning. Nature. 2015;**521**(7553):436-444

[9] Ranganathan H, Chakraborty S, Panchanathan S. Multimodal emotion recognition using deep learning architectures. in 2016 IEEE Winter Conference on Applications of Computer Vision (WACV). Lake Placid, NY, USA: IEEE; 2016

[10] He K et al. Deep Residual Learning for Image Recognition. In: 2016 IEEE Conference on Computer Vision and Pattern Recognition (CVPR). Las Vegas, NV, USA: IEEE; 2016

[11] Li B, Lima D. Facial expression recognition via ResNet-50. International Journal of Cognitive Computing in Engineering. 2021;**2**:57-64

[12] Kalaivani G, Sathyapriya S, Anitha DD. A literature review on emotion recognition for various facial emotional extraction. IOSR Journal of Computer Engineering. 2018:30-33

[13] Perez A. Recognizing human facial expressions with machine learning. 2018. Available from: https://thoughtworksarts.io/blog/recognizing-facial-expressions-machine-learning/

[14] Szegedy C et al. Going deeper with convolutions. In: Proceedings of the IEEE Conference on Computer Vision and Pattern Recognition. Boston, MA, USA: IEEE; 2015

[15] He K et al. Spatial pyramid pooling in deep convolutional networks for visual recognition. IEEE Transactions on Pattern Analysis and Machine Intelligence. 2015;**37**(9):1904-1916

[16] Team GL. Introduction to Resnet or Residual Network, in Great Learning Blog: Free Resources what Matters to shape your Career!; 2023. Available from: https://www.mygreatlearning.com/blog/resnet/

[17] He K, Sun J. Convolutional neural networks at constrained time cost. In: Proceedings of the IEEE Conference on Computer Vision and Pattern Recognition. Boston, USA: IEEE; 2015

[18] Han SS et al. Deep neural networks show an equivalent and often superior performance to dermatologists in onychomycosis diagnosis: Automatic construction of onychomycosis datasets by region-based convolutional deep neural network. PLoS One. 2018;**13**(1):e0191493

[19] Huang B et al. Identification and classification of aluminum scrap grades based on the Resnet18 model. Applied Sciences. 2022;**12**(21):1-16

[20] Wang S et al. Automatic detection and classification of steel surface defect using deep convolutional neural networks. Metals. 2021;**11**(3):388

[21] Ramzan F et al. A deep learning approach for automated diagnosis and multi-class classification of Alzheimer's disease stages using resting-state fMRI and residual neural networks. Journal of Medical Systems. 2020;**44**(2):1-16

[22] Ahonen T et al. Rotation invariant image description with local binary pattern histogram fourier features. In: Image Analysis. Berlin, Heidelberg: Springer; 2009

[23] Dammak S, Mliki H, Fendri E. Gender estimation based on deep learned and handcrafted features in an uncontrolled environment. Multimedia Systems. 2022;**Multimedia Systems**(1)

[24] Irhebhude AOK, Goma HK. A gender recognition system using facial images with high dimensional data Malaysian. Journal of Applied Sciences. 2021;**6**(1):27-45

[25] Bodapati JD, Veeranjaneyulu N. Facial emotion recognition using deep CNN based features. International Journal of Innovative Technology and Exploring Engineering. 2019;**8**(7):1928-1931

[26] Cai L et al. Audio-textual emotion recognition based on improved neural networks. Mathematical Problems in Engineering. 2019;**2019**(6):1-9

[27] Fei Y, Jiao G. Research on facial expression recognition based on voting model. In: IOP Conference Series: Materials Science and Engineering. Beijing, China: IOP Publishing; 2019

[28] Ansari AA, Singh AK, Singh A. Speech emotion recognition using CNN. International Research Journal of Engineering and Technology (IRJET). 2020;7(6):4302-4308

[29] Sujanaa J, Palanivel S, Balasubramanian M. Emotion recognition using support vector machine and one-dimensional convolutional neural network. Multimedia Tools and Applications. 2021;**80**(18):27171-27185

[30] Minaee S, Minaei M, Abdolrashidi A. Deep-emotion: Facial expression recognition using attentional convolutional network. Sensors. 2021;**21**(9):3046

[31] Shirisha K, Buddha M. Facial emotion detection using convolutional neural network. International Journal of Scientific & Engineering Research. 2020;**11**(3):51-55

[32] Kim JW, Saurous RA. Emotion recognition from human speech using temporal information and deep learning. In: INTERSPEECH. Hyderabad, India: ISCA Medal Talk; 2018

[33] Santhoshkumar R, Geetha MK. Deep Learning Approach for Emotion Recognition from Human Body Movements with Feedforward Deep

Convolution Neural Networks. Procedia Computer Science. 2019;**152**:158-165

[34] Selvapriya M, Maria GP. A review of classification methods for social emotion analysis. International Journal of Scientific Research in Computer Science Engineering and Information Technology. 2018;**3**(3):1737-1750

[35] Mohamed A. Comparative Study of Four Supervised Machine Learning Techniques for Classification. International Journal of Applied Science and Technology, 2017;**7**(2):5-18

[36] Luna-Jimenez C et al. A proposal for multimodal emotion recognition using aural transformers and action units on RAVDESS dataset. Applied Sciences. 2022;**12**(1):1-23

[37] Kaviya P, Arumugaprakash T. Group facial emotion analysis system using convolutional neural network. In: 2020 4th International Conference on Trends in Electronics and Informatics (ICOEI) (48184). Tirunelveli, India: IEEE; 2020

[38] Babajee P et al. Identifying human emotions from facial expressions with deep learning. In: 2020 Zooming Innovation in Consumer Technologies Conference (ZINC). Novi Sad, Serbia: IEEE; 2020. pp. 36-39

[39] Awatramani J, Hasteer N. Facial expression recognition using deep learning for children with autism spectrum disorder. In: 2020 IEEE 5th International Conference on Computing Communication and Automation (ICCCA). Greater Noida, India: IEEE; 2020

[40] Ahmad IS et al. Deep learning based on CNN for emotion recognition using EEG signal. WSEAS Transactions on Signal Processing. 2021;**17**:28-40

[41] Sandhu N, Malhotra A, Bedi MK. Human emotions detection using hybrid CNN approach. International Journal of Computer Science and Mobile Computing. 2020;**9**(10):1-9

[42] Santoso BE, Kusuma GP. Facial emotion recognition on FER2013 using VGGSPINALNET. Journal of Theoretical and Applied Information Technology. 2022;**100**(7):2008-2102

[43] Kabir HD et al. Spinalnet: Deep neural network with gradual input. IEEE Transactions on Artificial Intelligence. 2022;**03347**:1-10

[44] Chopra, P., Progressivespinalnet architecture for fc layers. arXiv preprint arXiv:2103.11373. 2021

[45] Bah I, Xue Y-Z. Facial expression recognition using adapted residual based deep neural network. Intelligence and Robotics. 2022;**2**(1):72-88

[46] Zhu D et al. Facial emotion recognition using a novel fusion of convolutional neural network and local binary pattern in crime investigation. Computational Intelligence and Neuroscience. 2022;**2022**:2249417

[47] Durga BK, Rajesh V. A ResNet deep learning based facial recognition design for future multimedia applications. Computers and Electrical Engineering. 2022;**104**:108384

[48] Irhebhude ME, Kolawole AO, Abdullahi F. Northern Nigeria human age estimation from facial images using rotation invariant local binary pattern features with principal component analysis. Egyptian Computer Science Journal. 2021;**45**(1):12-28

[49] Sanbare, M. FER-2013. 2020. Available from: https://www.kaggle.com/datasets/msambare/fer2013

[50] Zahara L et al. The facial emotion recognition (FER-2013) dataset for prediction system of micro-expressions face using the convolutional neural network (CNN) algorithm based raspberry Pi. In: 2020 Fifth International Conference on Informatics and Computing (ICIC). Gorontalo, Indonesia: IEEE; 2020. pp. 1-9

Chapter 2

Perspective Chapter: Emotion Detection Using Speech Analysis and Deep Learning

Alexander I. Iliev

Abstract

Speech reflects the sentiment and emotions of humans. People can identify the emotional states in speech utterances, but there is a higher chance of perception error, which is generally termed as human error to identify the proper emotion when only using speech signals. Thus, artificial intelligence plays an important role in the detection of emotion through speech. Deep Learning is the subset of Machine Learning (ML) and artificial intelligence through which speech signal processing can be performed and the detection of emotions can be accomplished using speech. In this chapter, the classifiers of Machine Learning and Deep Learning will be reviewed. From the comparison in various studies and performances we will conclude what methods work better than others. We will discuss the limitations of these approaches as well. Accuracy scores will be discussed for each proposed system.

Keywords: emotion recognition, emotional intelligence, speech analysis, deep learning, machine learning

1. Introduction

1.1 Paul Eckman

We are expressing our emotions through text, speech, songs, facial expressions, and body language. Recognizing emotions from text is gaining more and more popularity. Emotions expressed in terms of text are many times confusing and unexpected because they mostly depend on both context and language. The detection of human emotions from one's image or video recording then further classifying it into one of several emotion categories is still rather challenging task and many researchers proposed various methods to achieve this goal. The general framework of emotion detection through images is given in **Figure 1**. It may contain blocks such as: image preprocessing, face detection, facial landmark detection, feature vector creation, emotion classification, and finally the output of the system.

The first stage is used to remove noise present in the image, contrast adjustment and/or image resizing, if required. The second stage contains the detection of face from the given image and removing unwanted portion. In the third stage facial

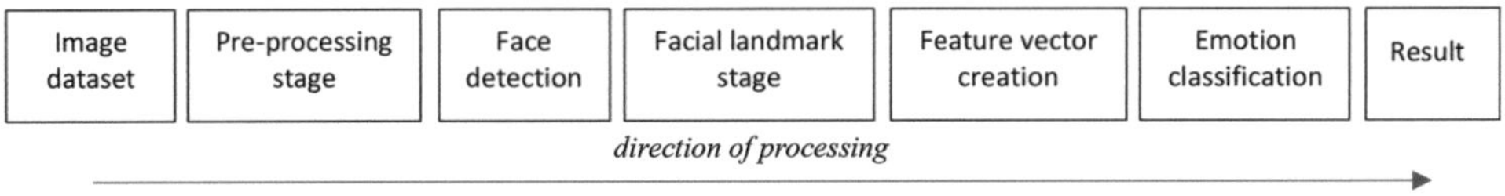

Figure 1.
General framework of emotion detection through images.

landmark detection takes place. This process includes eyes detection, nose detection, eyebrows detection, and hips detection. After detecting the landmarks, in the next stage feature vector is formed which is given to the last stage i.e., emotion classification. This stage outputs the category of the detected emotion in the given input image of a person.

Consistent with Don Hockenberry and Sandra E. Hockenberry, emotions can be thought of as a mentally complex phenomenon that involves three distinct psychological states, subject, response, and expression. But in 1972, Paul Ekman was able to classify these states into 6 different expressions that we call Emotions. He classifies them as:

- Fear
- Disgust
- Anger
- Surprise
- Happiness
- Sadness

He explains that emotions are a result of an automated response that is generated in reply to a speech or any form of information that has been relayed and was found important. These replies are influenced by our years of evolution and past experiences.

Simply put, emotions help us prepare for expected and unexpected events without even thinking about it. Although people are separated by various forms such as culture, language, and geographical boundaries, the 6 emotions mentioned here are what connect us and are believed to be expressed in the same way all over the world.

The image shown in **Figure 2** perfectly illustrates the different types of emotions that Paul Eckman has specified. There are various situations that can trigger any of the above-mentioned emotions. The situations can be:

- Any physical occurrence
- A social gathering
- Recurrence of nostalgic about any previous event
- Talking about an experience

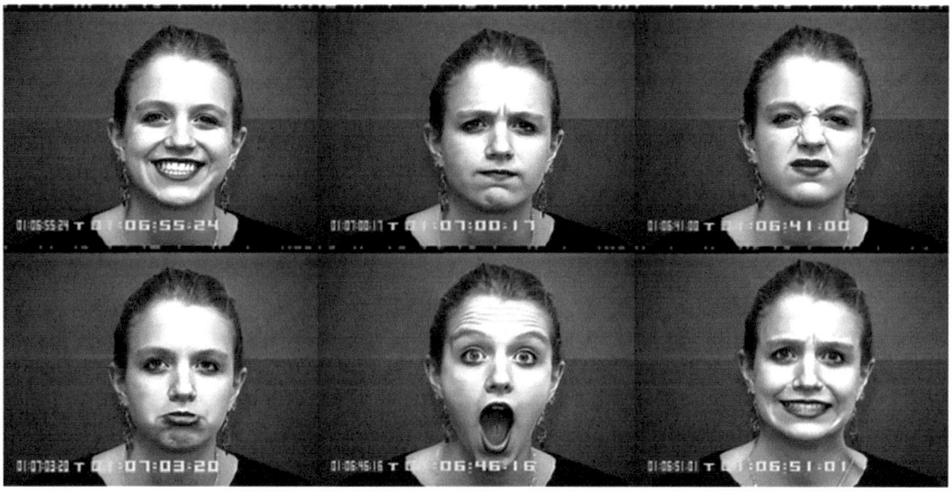

Figure 2.
Six different emotional states from top left to bottom right: Joy, anger, disgust, sadness, surprise, and fear [source: https://www.theatlantic.com/].

1.2 Robert Plutchik

Although these being the common factors, it does not stop here. It may vary person to person and an emotion expressed by one individual may or may not be the same as for another individual for the same given situation. However, Psychologist Robert Plutchik differentiated emotions in a more complex way. He derived the Plutchik model as shown in **Figure 3**.

In 1980, in reply to his early 2D model, Plutchik developed a 3D model of emotions. The wheel can be sought as a map to explain the various complexities associated with every emotion. He explains, emotions start out as simple, but depending on an individual's ethnic and socio-cultural background, can branch to various forms of other high level emotions. Further, he divides basic emotions in pair of two. They are:

- Sad and Joy
- Disgust and Trust
- Anticipation and Surprise
- Anger and Fear

Taking the help of the 3D wheel illustrated above, we can now divide these emotions to more complex ones.

- Joy + Anticipation = Optimism (Opposite: Disapproval)
- Trust + Joy = Love (Opposite: Remorse)
- Fear + Trust = Submission (Opposite: Contempt)
- Surprise + Fear = Awe (Opposite: Aggression)

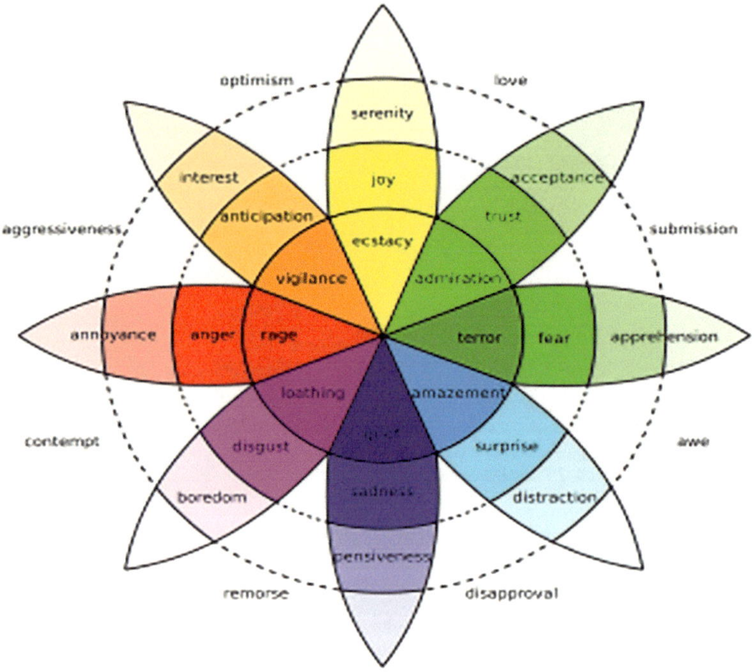

Figure 3.
Robert Plutchik 2D model [source: spring.co.uk].

- Surprise + Sadness = Disapproval (Opposite: Optimism)
- Sadness + Disgust = Remorse (Opposite: Love)
- Disgust + Anger = Contempt (Opposite: Submission)
- Anticipation + Anger = Aggressive (Opposite: Awe)

This wheel of emotion can be considered as a good starting point, but it also has its own limitations.

1.3 The importance of emotions

1.3.1 Expression of feelings

Brain performs some processes which help us associating a type of emotion to a kind of experience we are facing. From the smell of fresh baked bread to a late night horror show, various stimuli can elicit different emotional responses. This is one of the most important tasks the brain performs. It is also the main reason that we feel comfortable with certain situations and react accordingly. For example, listening to an old song makes us feel nostalgic and happy whereas listening to a sad song makes us sad. In today's world, it is very much said that to work and feel healthy, expressions of emotions are necessary. There are many benefits associated with it like,

- Helps solving long-standing problems,
- Decision-making gets easier,
- Depression is eased off,
- Anxiety reduces.

Failure to express emotions may have some detrimental effects too.

- A state of flight or fight.
- It puts a stress on our body.
- Increases heart rate and makes us depressed or anxious.

In research that was carried out in 2013–2014, the authors [1] help us understand how a particular individual is feeling on a given day of the week as well as in given time of the day. The participants particularly were given a questionnaire and told to be filled whenever they were experiencing a given set of emotions at any given time and day. Unsurprisingly, the participants faced the maximum number of emotions from 7 AM to 8 PM. This can be regarded to the fact that most of us are active during this time. Among emotions, Joy was particularly experienced by majority of the population followed by Love and Anxiety.

In another research, authors only focus on teenagers from United States who use social media. There are many comments and observations that can be inferred from the study, but the main points are as follows: around 25% of the teenagers felt less lonely while using social media apps whereas 21% felt more popular while using them. 20% of the people felt confident with themselves whenever they used various social media apps.

Both research papers give us a good idea of the important role emotions play in today's world. Further, we discuss about how globally important emotions are across cultures.

1.3.2 Emotions as a tool for globalization

A case study carried out in 2008 [2], explained various modes of communication between the Filipino staff and their Australian clients. Data generated was in the form of phone calls collected over period of months talked about how the cultural difference could have adverse effects on the success ratio of the staff and the approval ratings of the clients. Ultimately, it was concluded that if there was a good understanding of cultures between the staff, the ratings would have been better.

Due to globalization, there has a been a lot of interaction between various cultures. It becomes utmost important to carefully understand what the person in front is speaking to formulate response based on that. Misunderstanding may lead to unfortunate consequences.

Historically, Speech has been the greatest form of communication. World leaders, and great orators have time and again used speech to motivate and inspire the crowd. Emotions play a vital role in such situations and can have a positive impact on the crowd.

1.3.3 Emotional intelligence

Emotional intelligence is the ability to comprehend, organize emotions positively, to ease off the stress, communicate in a better way, relate to others, and fight difficult situations and relax conflicts. Emotional Quotient also is an important factor in building strong relationships, which brings success at home and office. It also helps to achieve personal milestones. According to a https://www.helpguide.org/ from July 2021 [3], emotional intelligence is mainly influenced by 3 factors.

- Self-Management: This is the ability to control strong feelings and manage our emotions in a better way.
- Self-Awareness: Able to understand our own emotions and how it has various effects on thoughts and processes.
- Managing Relationships: Can develop good and strong relationships which are long lasting.

1.4 Emotional Process

Another report published at University of Alabama [4], assesses emotion based on 3 factors.

1.4.1 Subjective experiences

Emotions are typically associated with past experiences and can be triggered by certain stimuli. Whether it is a familiar smell leading to a happy emotion or the loss of a loved one causing a more complex emotional response, individuals are always expressing one emotion or another. Moreover, the same experience can evoke an array of emotions across different individuals.

1.4.2 Physiological responses

Everyone has, at one time or another, felt their heart beating fast in situations such as waiting for expected results, which is often expressed as fear. When entering a new relationship, the feeling is often described as butterflies flying in the stomach.

1.4.3 Behavioral responses

This part talks about the actual expression of any emotion. They include anything from Smile, a sigh or laugh depending on situations. There has been numerous research undertaken that explains how facial expressions are universally expressed in the same way.

These expressions are very important to show how an individual is feeling to others, and they are also essential for one's wellbeing.

2. Emotion vs. mood

Affect is termed as general keyword used to describe a broad range of feelings experienced by people. It is a superficial concept that has both emotions and moods

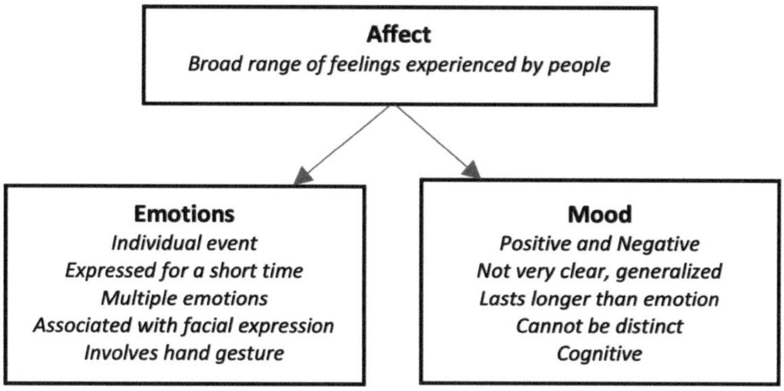

Figure 4.
Emotions vs. mood.

associated with it. Emotions are just some strong feelings experienced or expressed at someone. Mood is less intense and does not need a context to be true.

Many researchers have said that emotions are temporary as compared to moods. For example, if something goes wrong and not as expected by an individual, he/she will get angry but that anger feeling fades quickly. But if there is a bad mood, it will stay on for a longer period.

Emotions can be triggered by a situation or something someone has said, causing an individual to feel a range of emotions such as anger, happiness, or sadness. These are contextualized as strong feelings. Whereas mood is necessarily not expressed at a person. They might be the result of emotions not being resolved quickly. They generally happen when you lose concentration over a certain thing. For example, if a colleague questions you on the way an individual spoke to a client, that individual might get angry. You show emotion at a specific thing, but as that dissipates, your emotion gets generalized.

As **Figure 4** shows, affect is a highly generalized term. There are significant differences between Mood and Emotions. This image also describes how emotions and mood can influence each other. If an emotion is intense and stable enough, it can transform into a mood. Getting a job make us happy, and this feeling can last for several days. Similarly, if you are experiencing a positive or negative mood, you may feel strong positive or negative emotions in response to situations that arise at that moment.

Some aspects to be considered for emotion are:

- Intensity: Individuals give varied feelings for same emotional stimuli. There may be some people who almost never show any feelings. Those people rarely get angry. Also, there would be people who are highly emotional and show emotions all day long.

- Frequency and Period: Emotions cannot be expressed for a long period of time. Also, the emotional demands are too hard to maintain.

3. Speech analysis and properties

3.1 Properties of speech signal

The resonance architecture of the auditory tract, specifically the two bottom resonances known as formants, can be easily examined by drawing an "envelope" over the spectrum. This involves drawing a continuous line immediately above the spectrum, as shown in the picture on the right [5]. As a result, researchers receive the spectral envelope that describes the macro-shape of a voice signal's spectrum and is frequently used to describe speech signals. The basic frequency of a spoken transmission, or its lack thereof, conveys a great deal of information. Voiced and unvoiced parts of speech are those that have or do not have a vibration in the vocal cords. Researchers classify phonemes into voiceless or voiced categories based on their predominance. A speech signal with its spectral properties is shown in **Figure 5a** and **b** [6].

As mentioned in [6], when developing a speech processing system, data will be used for:

a. *Speech analysis* in order to observe the signal from speech production process. This way we can identify different properties of speech that can help us improve performance and increase our comprehension of features importance.

b. *Use Machine Learning* so that we can successfully train any given model for specific automation and smart development of subsequent systems.

c. *Performance evaluation* of the speech system. This stage is vast and can take different shapes and forms as it is developed for various needs. Therefore, the speech corpus must be such that can be used both in training, validation, and testing for the specific environment for which it is intended to be used.

A sample, limited-vocabulary speech recognition data for speech commands can be found in [7].

3.2 Speech linguistic structure

Several linguistic features of speech, including consonants and phrases, have written language equivalents. Nevertheless, it is critical to distinguish between the two: Speech signals always are uninterrupted and non-categorical, but written language is made up of discrete category pieces. This really is owing to the motor activity in speech generation, which acts in real time and at a limited pace while being constrained by physiological and neurophysiologic restrictions [8–10]. Therefore, the generated voice signal is similarly constant in time and frequency. Furthermore, since voice conveys additional data in regards of how items are spoken and the qualities of the speaker, recorded language is deficient in these areas. Written language, on the other hand, employs lexical and grammatical techniques, as well as unique characters, to distinguish finer-grained interpretations, such as communicating emotional content or distinguishing inquiries from assertions. The speech structure is shown in **Figure 6** [6].

3.3 Speech waveforms

The speech signals are categorized as audio or sound pulses that can travel from one place to another regarding the internal energy in it. The waveform of speech signals contains different components such as the frequency, magnitude, phase etc. In the present environment, we are particularly concerned with waveforms processing and analysis in digital systems. As a result, researchers would always presume that the acoustic voice signals were caught by a microphone and translated to digital format.

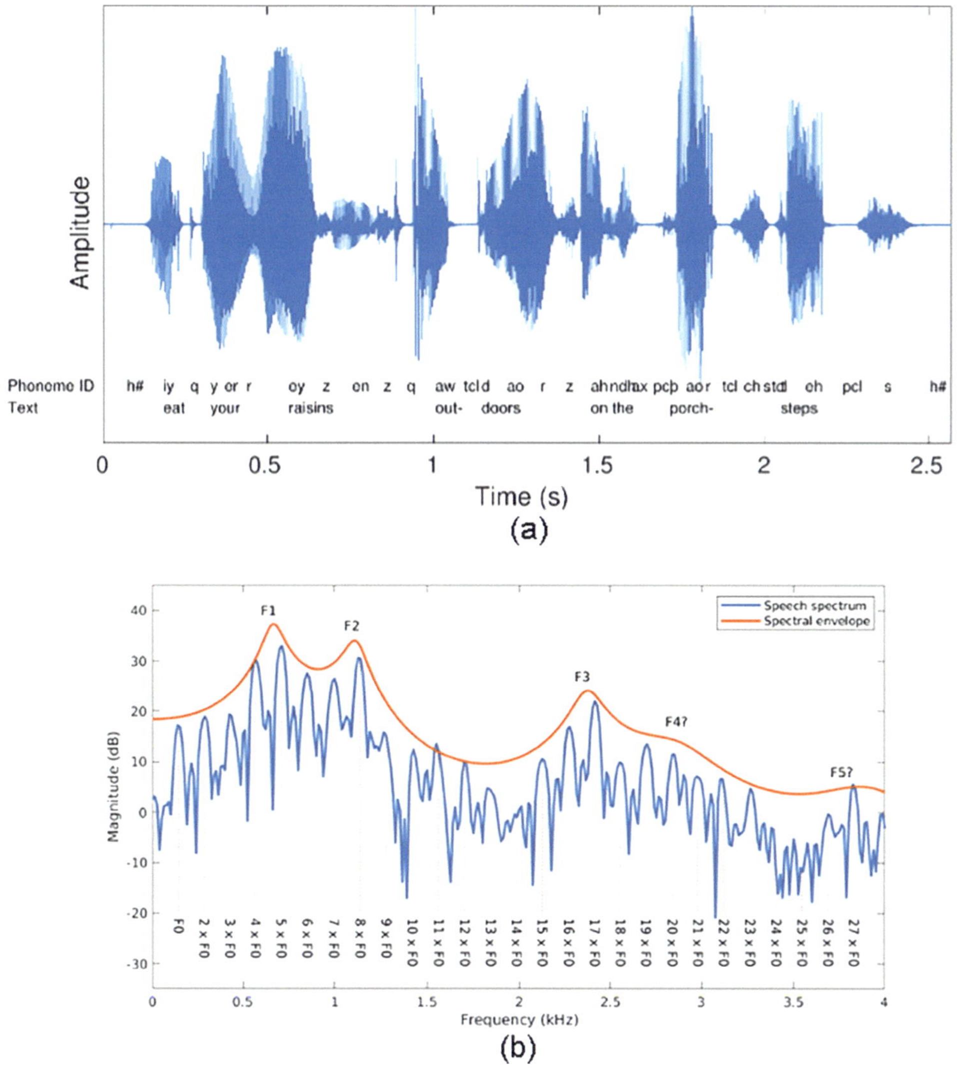

Figure 5.
(a) Speech signal in time domain [6] (b) Formants in a speech signal [6].

The consonants in speech signals contain crucial information, that ranges from 300 to 3500 Hz, implying that a lower threshold for sampling frequency is roughly 7 or 8 kHz [11]. Most power, though, stays below 8 kHz, implying that wide band, that really is, a sampling frequency of 16 kHz, is enough for most applications.

3.4 Speech signal windowing

Windowing of speech signals involves dividing or sub-sampling speech pulses into several short segments [12]. Windowing functions are seamless operations that return to zero at the edges. With the application of the windowing process, the audio signals can be truncated into pieces from which the overall features and properties of the speech signals can be identified rather than considering a long speech pulse. A simple window is shown in **Figure** 7 [6].

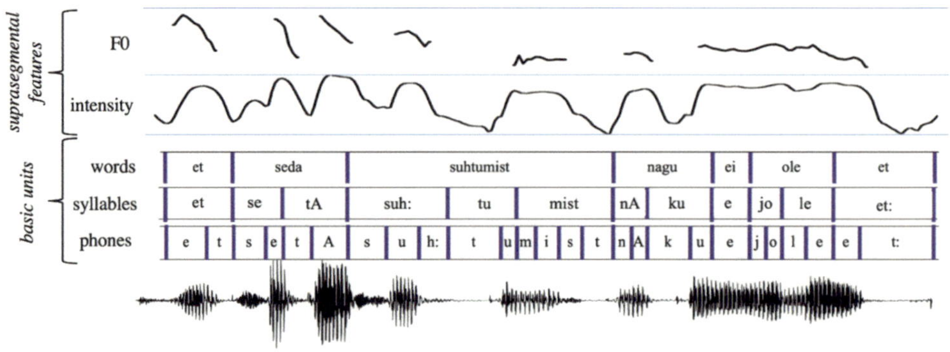

Figure 6.
Hierarchical organization of speech in terms of phones, syllables, and words [6].

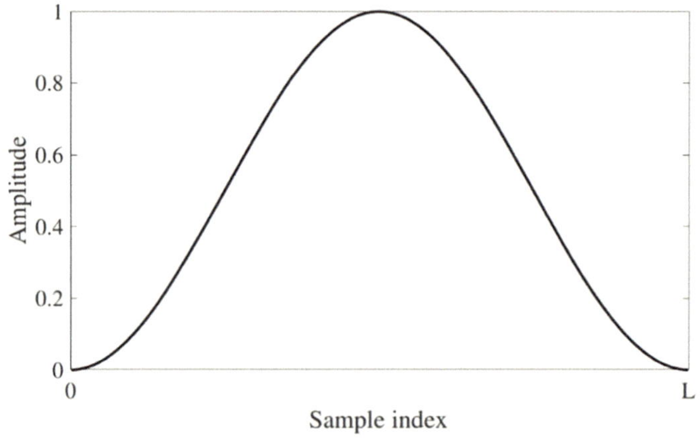

Figure 7.
Speech signal window [6].

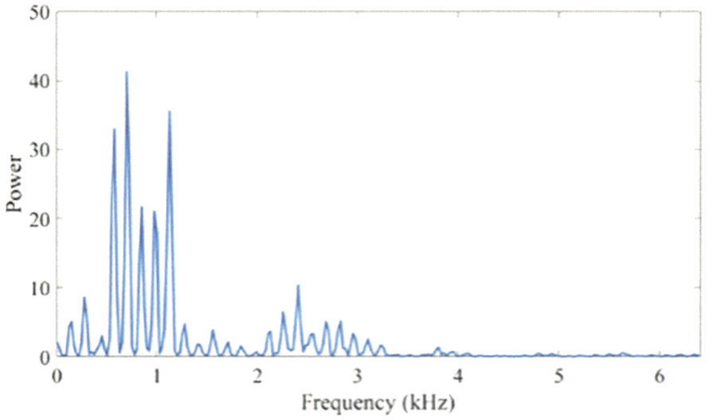

Figure 8.
Windowed speech signal [6].

In **Figure 8**, we see a window applied over a speech sample with its resulting signal in time and frequency domains respectively.

3.5 Speech spectrogram

Speech signals, on the other hand, are non-stationary indicators. When we convert a spoken phrase to the frequency response, then get a spectrum that is an aggregate of all phonemes in the phrase, although we typically want to view the spectrum of every single phoneme independently [12]. Researchers can concentrate on signal qualities at a certain point in time by dividing the information into shorter parts. This type of segmentation already was covered in the windowing part. One of the most utilized techniques in speech processing and analysis is the Short-Time Fourier Transform (STFT). It illustrates how frequency components change over time. One of the advantages of STFTs is that its characteristics have a simple physiological and understandable explanation.

3.6 Speech cestrum and Mel-frequency cepstral coefficient (MFCC)

Cestrum refers to the properties of the speech signals that help detect the information of the speech signal [12]. It can be obtained by extracting the features from the speech signals so that the essential components of the speech audio can be identified [6]. This component can be extracted using the application of speech processing and the Mel-Frequency Cepstral Coefficient (MFCC) method where the cepstral components are achieved through numerical data. This is essential in Machine Learning and Deep Learning as the algorithms require numerical features to classify and detect the type of speech and to identify the emotions.

4. Speech emotion detection using machine learning

According to Qing and Zhong [13], the rise of big data handling in recent times, coupled with the continual improvement of computers' computational power and the ongoing improvement of techniques, has led to significant advancements in the field. Also, with the advancement of artificial intelligence studies, individuals are not always content that the computer does have the same problem-solving abilities as the human mind. Still, they also wish for a much more humanized artificial intelligence with the same emotions and character. It may be utilized in students' learning to recognize students' feelings in real time and analyze them appropriately and in intelligent human-computer interaction to detect the speaker's emotional shifts in real time. Researchers primarily investigate the Mel-Cepstral Coefficient settings and K-Nearest Neighbor algorithm (KNN) for speech signals and implement MFCC extraction of features using MATLAB and emotion classification using the KNN method. The CASIA corpus is utilized for training and validation, and it eventually achieved 78% accuracy. As per Kannadaguli and Bhat [14], humans see feelings as physiological changes in the composition of consciousness caused by various ideas, sentiments, sensations, and actions. Although emotions vary with an individual's familiarity, they remain consistent with attitude, color, character, and inclination. Researchers employ Bayesian and Hidden Markov Model (HMM) based techniques to study and assess the effectiveness of speaker-dependent emotion identification systems. Because all emotions may not have the same prior probability, researchers must calculate the conditional probability by multiplying the pattern's chances by each class's previous distribution and dividing by the pattern's likelihood function derived by summing its potential for all categories. An emotion-based information model is constructed using the acoustic-phonetic modeling technique to voice recognition. Following that, the template classifier and pattern recognition are built using the three probabilistic methodologies in Machine Learning.

As described by Nasrun and Setianingsih [15], emotions in daily language are often associated with feelings of anger or rage experienced by an individual. Nevertheless, the fact that action is predisposed as a property of emotions does not necessarily make things simpler to describe terminologically. Speech is a significant factor in determining one's psychological response. The Mel-Frequency Cepstral Coefficient (MFCC) approach, which involves extracting features, is commonly used in human emotion recognition system that are based on sound inputs. Support Vector Machine (SVM) is a novel data categorization approach developed in the 1990s. SVM is guided Machine Learning, frequently used in various research to categorize human voice recognition. The RBF kernel has been the most often used kernel in SVM multi-Class. This is because SVM employs the Radial Basis Function (RBF) seed to improve accuracy. This report's most incredible accuracy ratio was 72.5%.

According to Mohammad and Elhadef [16], emotion recognition in speech may be defined as perceiving and recognizing emotions in human communication. In other respects, speech- emotion perception means communicating with feelings between a computer and a human. The proposed methodology comprises three major phases: signal pre-processing to remove noise and decrease signal throughput, feature extraction using a combination of Linear Predictive Rules and 10-degree polynomial Curve fitting Coefficients over the periodogram power spectrum feature of the speech signal, and Machine Learning that utilizes various machine learning algorithms and compares their overall accuracy to determine the best accuracy. Several of the causes are that the recognition approach selects the best elements for a method to be powerful enough to distinguish between different emotions. Another factor is the variety of languages, dialects, phrases, and speaking patterns. As per Bharti and Kekana [17], speech conveys information and meaning via pitch, speech, emotion, and numerous aspects of the Human Vocal System (HVS). Researchers suggested an outline that recognizes sentiments using Speech Signal (SS) with the highest average accuracy and effectiveness when compared to techniques such as Hidden Markov Model and Support Vector Machine. The detection step can be easily implemented on various mobile platforms with minimal computing effort, as compared to previous approaches. The ML model has been trained successfully using the Multi-class Support Vector Machine (MSVM) approach to distinguish emotional categories based on selected features. In machine learning, Support Vector Machines (SVMs) are popular models used for classification and regression analysis. They're especially known for their effectiveness in high-dimensional spaces. However, traditional SVMs are inherently binary classifiers. When there are more than two classes in the dataset, adaptations like MSVMs are used, which can handle multi-class classification problems. The MSVM classification was used to extract features Gammatone Frequency Cepstral Coefficients (GFCC) and remove elements to achieve a high success rate of 97% on the RAVDESS data set (ALO). The GFCC is a feature extraction method used often in the field of speech and audio processing. The GFCC features try to mimic the human auditory system, capturing the phonetically important characteristics of speech, and are robust against noise. Whenever extracted features using MFCC are applied to existing databases, all classifiers achieve an accuracy of 79.48%.

As described by Gopal and Jayakrishnan [18], emotions are a very complicated psychological phenomenon that must be examined and categorized. Psychologists and neuroscientists have performed extensive studies to analyze and classify human emotions over the last two decades. Emotional prosody is used in several works. The goal of this project was to develop a mechanism for annotating novel texts with appropriate emotion. With the SVM classifier, a supervised method was used. The One-Against-Rest technique was utilized in a multi-class SVM architecture. The suggested approach would categorize Malayalam phrases into several emotion classes such as joyful, sad, angry, fear, standard, etc., using suitable level data with an overall accuracy of 91.8%. Throughout feature vector choice, many aspects such as n-grams, semantic orientation, POS-related features, and contextual details are analyzed to determine if the phrase is conversational, or a question.

5. Predictive visual analysis of speech data using machine learning algorithms

Goyal and Rathore [19] state that there is a vast amount of digital and social media data available on the internet, including platforms like Twitter, LinkedIn, message boards, blogging sites, customer groups, and feedback on products. In the modern environment, product feedback has become quite vital. The specific approaches, such as Max Monitoring, SVM, Naive Bayes, logistic regression, or KNN classification, can be used to detect faces and classify the displayed mood. The approaches mentioned here are utilized for document-level categorization. In this study, we apply the ME-based text technique to examine the level sense of neural networks using recursive nerve sensor networks that evaluate emotion at the phrase level. According to the investigation, real.

emotion, including audio and video, is identified by specific words with a sentiment component. This study lays the groundwork for future research to concentrate on phrases that influence decision-making and discover generic public mass assessments.

According to Ali et al. [20], there are numerous methods to define microaggressions (MAs). Derogatory stereotype representations that are "put setbacks" by such an offender often are subtle, shocking, frequently reflexive, and nonverbal encounters. Computerized MA detection introduces a new and difficult topic in Natural Language Processing (NLP) research and sentiment evaluation. A better understanding of how machine algorithms are constructed and how MAs are categorized in writing can help to enhance our understanding of sentiment in documents. Regarding MA identification, the outcomes of the two classification tests were encouraging. The characteristics recovered from the annotated dataset reinforce this point, with phrases/attributes that can be seen as slightly racist, such as darkish and minority, being picked in the first 20. There are not very harsh or obscene words/blasphemes on the listing. While employing these parameters, advancements in classification accuracy have also shown encouraging outcomes, with similar trends throughout all systems examined.

As stated by Tasha et al. [21], an emotion detection element could be added to spoken conversation systems. It can be used as a component of the interaction program's architecture to impact the interaction program's responsiveness to the customer's verbal statements or to improve the user interface in those other ways. The traditional GMM technique has the worst efficiency of 38%. Correspondingly, using a DNN or an ELM to assign various values to distinct characteristics improves accuracy to 48 and 51.6%. The DNN-ELMK algorithm continues to be the highest performer, with 57.9% accuracy. Researchers measured the effectiveness of numerous GMM-based algorithms that calculate the statistics of the complete speech first and then do classification, to our cutting-edge DNN-ELMK technique, which conducts a variety of segments first and then computes statistics. Ultimately, GMM-based algorithms cannot match the accuracy of the DNN-ELMK approach when showing emotion identification on 0.25-second components.

6. Speech emotion detection using deep learning

According to Tariq et al. [22], speech emotion detection has received a lot of interest in recognizing people's emotional states. Speech is an excellent mode of communication for identifying the speakers and many sorts of feelings. Researchers created an IoT system that predicts patients' moods in real time. Researchers used the SED model on actual data.

They discovered that female audio has a higher accuracy of 78% than male performers, who have an accuracy of 71% owing to the purity of their voices. They saw that their network was running quite well. We employed a 2D CNN model using Peak, RMS, and EBU normalization and data augmentation approach to train and test speech emotion detection. They discovered that combining the normalization and augmentation approaches acquired the greatest accuracy, superior to state-of-the-art techniques in audio-based emotions categorization and forecasting.

As stated by Zhang et al. [23], being one of the greatest natural forms of human interaction, speech signals include not just explicit language information but also implicitly paralinguistic data about the speaker. The suggested technique is tested on four available datasets: the Berlin database of the RML audio-visual dataset, German emotional speech (EMO-DB), the eNTERFACE05 audio-visual dataset, and the BAUM-1 s audio-visual set of data. Researchers offer a new automated emotional feature learning technique that combines DCNNs with DTPM. A DCNN is being used to train discriminative segment-level characteristics from triple channels of log Mel-spectrograms, analogous to RGB picture representations. DTPM is intended to combine learned segment-level elements into a universal utterance-level feature extraction for emotion identification.

According to Singh and Sharma [24], sentiments are "strong sentiments arising from one's surroundings, mood, or interactions with others." Emotions are the most important aspect of human communication in everyday life. Deep Learning approaches surpass shallow classifiers because external classifiers can only acquire high-level characteristics, but Deep Learning methods can develop insights through low-level information. There is a significant increase in accuracy from the SVM approach (86.75) to the LSTM approach (91.75). The CNN design with a two-layer deep network produces the greatest results (95.4%). Generally, SVM has the greatest outcomes in shallow structures. Deep Learning feeds on large amounts of data and would operate considerably better with large amounts of data.

As stated by An and Shi [25], due to urbanization and industrialization, social rivalry is rising in economic building and automation, leading to a dramatic increase in different psychological sources of stress, mental diseases, and mental health issues. A CNN architecture consists of six layers, including two convolution layers, two max-pooling layers, and two fully connected layers. The negative repercussions of a mental health issue are often dramatic and result in outrageous conduct. The testing set included 198 statements written by students with negative feelings and individuals with neutral feelings.

The findings indicated that the training model's accuracy was 78.4%, the test set's accuracy was 70.5%, and the final model's experimental outcomes were more than 70.5%.

According to Mokonyane and Sefira [26], Deep Learning is a Machine Learning approach that mimics the human brain's operations in the analysis of organized and unstructured information for application areas such as translation software, voice recognition, object identification, and many others. Deep Learning techniques may think of making judgments without human intervention. Researchers discovered that the Sigmoid Kernel fails to meet state-of-the-art accuracy, coming in last at 58%, followed by polynomial, linear, and RBF kernels, which achieved state-of-the-art accuracy at 81%, 85%, and 88%, correspondingly. After evaluating the models, deep neural networks outperformed Machine Learning methods in emotional speaker recognition from voice signals, achieving the most excellent accuracy of 92% and beating state-of-the-art designs.

As stated by Qidwai and Al-Meer [27], human emotion is crucial in human-human interaction since it conveys the person's unspoken mood. A CNN is typically composed of three layers: convolution, pooling, and fully linked layers. In CNN, the feature extractors are the convolution and pooling layers. A series of filters are convolved with the input picture in the convolution layer to extract features like vertical or horizontal lines. Emotion recognition garnered interest in human-centered design as computer technology advanced, particularly in Human-Computer Interaction. The suggested model obtains an overall accuracy of 81% on unseen data. Accordingly, it recognizes positive and negative feelings with 87% and 85% accuracy. The accuracy at distinguishing neutral emotion, on the other hand, is just 51%.

According to Gunathilake et al. [28], recently, text-to-speech synthesis has been challenging since the voices produced by these algorithms sound robotic and thus are easily distinguished from human agents. Despite extensive study into creating natural-sounding voices, delivering an emotional speech is a reasonably young topic. Expressive TTS has several uses, such as supporting the visually challenged, and emotion recognition from text is a critical module in this process. The technique of detecting emotions begins with identifying what emotions are. Researchers combine bi-directional long-short memories with an attention layer for higher prediction accuracy. To enhance future outcomes, researchers use text preparation. Researchers run the tests on three different data sets, as well as the algorithms are graded based on their classification results.

As stated by Lin and Yang [29], because of the rapid progress of Machine Learning and deep understanding in recent years, studies on using these technologies to aid in elderly care and children have become widespread. This research offers an intelligent system for distinguishing emotional sounds such as laugh, weep, scream, wail, or sigh to help caretakers comprehend the needs of the elderly and kids. They can receive appropriate care more rapidly. Empirical mode segmentation is utilized to improve the identification and recognition of emotional sounds. Furthermore, deep ensemble learning is used to address the issue of overfitting. Experiments reveal that the suggested technique has a classification accuracy of 91.6%, which is significantly higher than without using EMD. Researchers think that this technology will improve the care of the aged and young. According to Wani and Guna Wan [30], speech emotion recognition is an expanding topic of research currently, and as a result, multiple researchers have developed different technologies in this field. This procedure is required to categorize a voice signal to detect a specific mood. Many people strive to discover aspects of voice signals that range from efficient to salient to discriminative. The algorithms were fed spectrograms created from the speech dataset. As the number of test epochs increased from 500 to 1200 and 1500, the efficiency of both models improved. The provided model Depthwise Separable Convolutional Neural Networks (DSCNN) surpasses the current state-of-the-art model CNN by a wide margin. DSCNN achieved an accuracy of 87.8%, while CNN attained an accuracy of 79.4%. DSCNN is a variant of the standard convolutional neural network (CNN) and is part of the family of convolutional networks which are designed to be more efficient.

In a DSCNN, the convolution operation is split into two separate operations aiming to reduce the model's complexity and size. The first is a depthwise convolution which applies a single filter per input channel. The second is a pointwise convolution, a simple 1x1 convolution, which is used to build new features through computing linear combinations of the input channels.

This structure is a key element of several efficient and compact network architectures such as MobileNet developed by Google, which is used for tasks like object detection and image segmentation on mobile and embedded devices where computational resources are limited. More work is required to enhance the provided architecture for convincingly recognizing emotions.

7. Contributions and summary

As evident from the facts given, it is clear how important emotions are in our day to day lives. Globalization across the world has accelerated the need for better understanding of emotions. The interactions between various cultures at such a fast pace underlines the importance of expressing ourselves and our intentions to the crowd for maximum effect. Good orators and leaders have always used emotions to drive home their views and have a positive impact on their followers.

Numerous research has been undertaken to understand how important emotions are. They are explained by the multiple case studies discussed in the previous chapters. It is worth to note that emotions can have both positive and negative impact on our health. Thus, researchers advice that an individual should always express emotions from time to time to avoid depression and anxiety. In professional life, understanding your colleague from other country or culture helps in better communication and leads to increased success.

Therefore, we can see how emotions have played a vital role in all aspects of life. Going forward, we see the emergence of AI and how it helps to understand and express emotions even better.

The main contributions of this chapter are that it summarizes the latest state of the art in emotion recognition through various use case in different environments. A short summary is provided next:

8. Machine learning

Machine learning is a branch of AI that makes applications to have better and accurate predictions without hard coding it to do so. It uses historical data to predict new values. Common use cases include recommendation engines, credit detection, fraud, predictive maintenance.

It is necessary as it gives extended view of various behaviors and patterns as well as supporting new products. Almost all corporate giants like Google, Microsoft, IBM, Uber use ML as a core part of its operations. It has become so important to gain advantage over other companies, ML is seen as a solution. There are various types of Machine Learning:

- *Supervised Learning*: In this method, labeled historical data is given based on which models train and learn to associate various results. Then a user provides unseen data and based on metrics, we understand how accurate the model is.

- *Unsupervised Learning*: This type is totally opposite to Supervised learning. The model trains on unlabeled data and learns to associate results on its own. It looks for meaningful results and gives out relevant output.

- *Semi-Supervised Learning*: This is a combination of the two previous types. Some labeled data maybe be given as well as unlabeled data. In this, the model is free to make its own assumptions and give out results.

- *Reinforcement Learning*: The model starts by making a few predictions and outcomes. The user based on what results it receives gives out incentives or positive and negative reactions. The models take in the feedback given by the user and the future predictions are reliant on such feedbacks.

9. Machine learning use cases

The supervised machine learning can be used for a variety of tasks and will require labeled data to give outputs. The various tasks are:

- Binary Classification

- Multi-Class Classification

- Regression Technique

- Ensembling Technique

The unsupervised machine learning does not require labeled data. They analyze unlabeled data to identify patterns that can be utilized to classify data into various categories. Almost all Deep Learning techniques are unsupervised learning techniques. The various tasks for which unsupervised learning technique could be used are.

- Clustering

- Dimension Reduction techniques

- Associate

Reinforcement learning has a set of rules to accomplish a particular goal. DSs use algorithms with positive rewards, meaning when a model performs an action which leads to the goal, it gets a reward and when it performs badly, it leads to punishment. Such learning is often used in areas like.

- Resource management
- Videogames
- Robotics

As we can see, ML is used for a variety of reasons. One of the most famous examples is the recommendation engine employed by Netflix. Based on search results and movies an individual has seen, Netflix is able to suggest some other movies or shows for that individual. Other ways we can use ML is:

- *Customer Relationship Management systems (CRM)*: Based on importance of certain notifications, it tells the sales team to answer to important notifications first. A more complex system can also suggest the type of response.
- *Business Intelligence (BI)* and its analytic sellers use ML to analyze important data, see the trends and various deviations.
- *Chatbots*: They usually employ supervised as well as unsupervised learning techniques to give out curated results to the customers coming on the websites.

Advantages and Disadvantages of ML methods are summarized in **Table 1**.

As ML grows in demand, new techniques and applications will surface. Today's models need intense work before it gets optimized for one task. Some researchers are performing various operations to make ML models that are flexible and inexpensive with requiring low infrastructure. It will be not quick but once achieved, can pave way for more accurate and better results. A ML model generally goes through a common lifecycle as explained below.

- Data Collection
- Choosing a ML technique
- Finetuning
- Final model

9.1 Deep learning

It is a ML technique that makes computer learn things that a human can do naturally. It is the driving force behind many tasks which could be termed as complex for machines. Tasks such as self-driving cars, recognizing stop signal, drive in a straight

Advantages	Disadvantages
Help analyze customer behaviors.	Expensive
Customized product	High salaries for DS
Primary source for products	High infrastructure

Table 1.
Advantages and disadvantages of ML.

line and avoid collision. It also can be used for various control devices. DL can achieve better accuracy than classic ML algorithms. This helps in meeting various customer demands. Recent advancement has been so much that it outperforms humans in tasks like classification of objects.

Despite being discovered earlier, it has only achieved success in recent times. The reason being

- It requires large amount of labeled data.
- It requires a very high computing power.

There are various types of Deep Learning networks available in the market. Some of them are listed below.

- *Feed Forward Neural Network*: It is a basic kind of network in which data flows from one layer to another. It has only one kind of layer or just a hidden layer. There are no backpropagation techniques available. The weight sum is fed as an input to the next layer.
- *Radial-Basis Function (RBF) Neural Networks*: They have more than one type of layer. In such networks, the distance between any point to the center is calculated and passed as an input to the next layer.
- *Multi-Layer Perceptron*: It has multiple layers and used to classify non-linear data. They have fully connected layers.
- *Convolutional Neural Network (CNN)*: It has n number of layers. It can have more than one convolutional layer and is very deep with few parameters.
- *Recurrent Neural Network (RNN)*: An output from a particular neuron is fed as an input to the same node. It helps in getting better output. It has memory storage and utilizes past results to optimize future outcomes.
- *Modular Neural Network*: Such networks are a collection of smaller neural networks. Combination of smaller networks leads to a big neural network and all networks work independently to achieve results.
- *Sequence to Sequence models*: There are generally a combination of RNN networks. It works on encoding and decoding.

9.2 Deep learning use cases

- Speech Recognition
- Image Recognition
- Natural Language Processing
- Recommender Systems
- Customer Relationship Management systems

Advantages	Disadvantages
Features are finetuned automatically	Require large amount of data
Same network used for various tasks	Expensive
Flexible and can be adapted for various problems.	No tool to formulate correct neural network models

Table 2.
Advantages and disadvantages of DL.

Advantages and Disadvantages of Deep Learning methods are summarized in **Table 2**. The Deep Learning lifecycle is like the one used for Machine Learning.

- Collection of Data
- Creation of model
- Training of model
- Deploying

Author details

Alexander I. Iliev[1,2,3]

1 Institute of Mathematics and Informatics, Bulgarian Academy of Sciences, Sofia, Bulgaria

2 SRH University Berlin, Charlottenburg, Germany

3 UC Berkeley, Berkeley, California, USA

*Address all correspondence to: ailiev@berkeley.edu

References

[1] Trampe D, Quoidbach J, Taquet M. Emotions in everyday life. PloS One. 2015;**10**(12):e0145450

[2] Owens A. A Case study of cross-cultural communication issues for Filipino call centre staff and their Australian customers. In: 2008 IEEE International Professional Communication Conference. Montreal: IEEE; 2008. pp. 1-10

[3] Jeanne Segal PM. 2021. articles. Retrieved from: https://www.helpguide.org/articles/mental-health/emotional-intelligence-eq.htm#

[4] Australia, U. The Science of Emotion: Exploring The Basics Of Emotional Psychology. 2019. Retrieved from: https://online.uwa.edu/news/emotional-psychology/

[5] Backstrom T. Speech Production and Acoustic Properties. Aalto University; 2021. Available from: https://speechprocessingbook.aalto.fi/

[6] Aalto. Speech Processing. [Online]. 2020. Available on Jan.10.2023 at: https://wiki.aalto.fi/display/ITSP/Introduction+to+Speech+Processing

[7] Warden P. Speech Commands: A Dataset for Limited-Vocabulary Speech Recognition. DOI: 10.48550/arXiv.1804.03209

[8] Blanding M. The role of emotions in effective negotiations. 2014. Retrieved from: https://hbswk.hbs.edu/item/the-role-of-emotions-in-effective-negotiation

[9] Pavelescu LM, Petrić B. Studies in second language learning and teaching. 2018. Retrieved from: https://pressto.amu.edu.pl/index.php/ssllt

[10] Raisanen O. Linguistic Structure of Speech. Aalto University; 2021. Available from: https://speechprocessingbook.aalto.fi/

[11] Backstrom T. Waveform. Aalto University; 2022. Available from: https://speechprocessingbook.aalto.fi/

[12] Backstrom T. Windowing. Spectrogram and the STFT, Cestrum and MFCC: Aalto University; 2019. Available from: https://speechprocessingbook.aalto.fi/

[13] Qing Z, Zhong W. Research on speech emotion recognition technology based on machine learning. In: 7th International Conference on Information Science and Control Engineering (ICISCE). 2020. pp. 1220-1223

[14] Kannadaguli P, Bhat V. A comparison of Bayesian and HMM based approaches in machine learning for emotion detection in native Kannada speaker. In: IEEMA Engineer Infinite Conference (TechNet). 2018. pp. 1-6

[15] Nasrun M, Setianingsih C. Human emotion detection with speech recognition using Mel-frequency cepstral coefficient and support vector machine. In: International Conference on Artificial Intelligence and Mechatronics Systems (AIMS). 2021. pp. 1-6

[16] Mohammad OA, Elhadef M. Arabic speech emotion recognition method based on LPC and PPSD. In: 2nd International Conference on Computation, Automation and Knowledge Management (ICCAKM). 2021. pp. 31-36

[17] Bharti D, Kekana P. A hybrid machine learning model for emotion recognition from speech signals. In:

International Conference on Smart Electronics and Communication (ICOSEC). 2020. pp. 491-496

[18] Gopal GN, Jayakrishnan R. Multi-class emotion detection and annotation in Malayalam Novels. In: International Conference on Computer Communication and Informatics (ICCCI). 2018. pp. 1-5

[19] Goyal N, Rathore SS. Predictive visual analysis of speech data using machine learning algorithms. In: 3rd International Conference on Emerging Technologies in Computer Engineering: Machine Learning and Internet of Things (ICETCE). 2020. pp. 69-73

[20] Ali O et al. Automated Detection of Racial Microaggressions Using Machine Learning. IEEE; 2020

[21] Tasha IJ, Wang Z-Q, Godin K. Speech emotion recognition based on Gaussian mixture models and deep neural networks. In: 2017 Information Theory and Applications Workshop (ITA). 2017

[22] Tariq Z, Shah SK, Lee Y. Speech emotion detection using IoT based deep learning for health care. In: 2019 IEEE International Conference on Big Data (Big Data). 2019. pp. 4191-4196

[23] Zhang S, Zhang S, Huang T, Gao W. Speech emotion recognition using deep convolutional neural network and discriminant temporal pyramid matching. IEEE Transactions on Multimedia. 2018:1576-1590

[24] Singh V, Sharma K. Empirical analysis of shallow and deep architecture classifiers on emotion recognition from speech. In: 2019 6th IEEE International Conference on Cyber Security and Cloud Computing (Cloud)/ 2019 5th IEEE International Conference on Edge Computing and Scalable Cloud (Edgecam). 2019. pp. 69-73

[25] An H, Shi D. Mental health detection from speech signal: A convolution neural networks approach. In: International Joint Conference on Information, Media, and Engineering (IJCIME). 2019. pp. 436-439

[26] Mokonyane TB, Sefira TJ. Emotional speaker recognition based on machine and deep learning. In: 2nd International Multidisciplinary Information Technology and Engineering Conference (IMITEC). 2020. pp. 1-8

[27] Qidwai U, Al-Meer M. Emotional stability detection using convolutional neural networks. In: IEEE International Conference on Informatics, IoT, and Enabling Technologies (Ikot). 2020. pp. 136-140

[28] Gunathilake S, Raj U. Emotion detection using Bi-directional LSTM with an effective text pre-processing method. In: 12th International Conference on Computing Communication and Networking Technologies (ICCCNT). 2021. pp. 1-4

[29] Lin Y-Y, Yang J-Y. Use empirical mode decomposition and ensemble deep learning to improve the performance of emotional voice recognition. In: IEEE 2nd International Workshop on System Biology and Biomedical Systems (SBBS). 2020. pp. 1-4

[30] Wani TM, Guna Wan TS. Speech emotion recognition using convolution neural networks and deep stride convolutional neural networks. In: 6th International Conference on Wireless and Telematics (ICWT). 2020. pp. 1-6

Chapter 3

Application of Machine and Deep Learning Techniques to Facial Emotion Recognition in Infants

Uma Maheswari Pandyan, Mohamed Mansoor Roomi Sindha, Priya Kannapiran, Senthilarasi Marimuthu and Vinora Anbunathan

Abstract

Infant facial expression recognition is one of the most significant areas of research in the field of computer vision and surveillance parental care. It is essential for both the early diagnosis of medical conditions and intelligent interpersonal interactions. Despite recent improvements in face detection, feature extraction techniques, and expression categorization methods, it is still difficult to develop an automated system employing deep learning methods that achieves the goal of recognizing infant emotions. The prime aim of this chapter is to present a comprehensive framework for recognizing infant emotions using machine learning and deep learning algorithms on the dataset for infant emotions currently accessible. The proposed model directs future research on early detection of infant emotions and has the ability to identify emotional-related medical problems. This article will incorporate the findings on infant emotion recognition required to address the parental supervision and enhance intelligent interpersonal relationships.

Keywords: infant emotion recognition, machine learning, deep learning, facial emotion, surveillance parental care

1. Introduction

Facial expressions, which are a vital aspect of communication, are one of the most important ways humans communicate facial expressions. There is a lot to comprehend about the messages we transmit and receive through nonverbal communication, even when nothing is said explicitly. Nonverbal indicators are vital in interpersonal relationships, and facial expressions communicate them. There are seven universal facial expressions that are employed as nonverbal indicators: laugh, cry, fear, disguise, anger, contempt, and surprise.

From the moment of birth, babies can convey their interest, pain, disgust, and enjoyment through their body language and facial expressions. Around 2–3 months old, babies start smiling spontaneously, and around 4 months old, they start laughing. Although your infant may make eye contact with you, itis likely that crying will be the predominant behavior your baby exhibits. For instance, your baby may scream just because they want to be cuddled or because they are hungry, upset, wet, or uncomfortable.

Facial expressions are one of the key methods that infants communicate their needs and emotions. As a result, it's critical to comprehend their facial expressions and pay attention to them in order to provide appropriate treatment. Understanding their emotions is essential for early diagnosis and treatment of diseases like Autism Spectrum Disorder (ASD) and Attention-Deficit Hyperactivity Disorder (ADHD). Empirical evidence suggests that early intervention for certain problems affects children's development in the long run.

Recently, the field of computer vision has accorded facial emotion recognition a lot of attention. However, adult facial expressions are the main focus of the research. Adult and newborn face structures differ from one another. Infants have rounder faces, eyes that are closer together and much bigger, shorter lips, and lips that resemble a "cupid bow." Their faces feature big fat pads and elastic skin, which prevents folds and wrinkles while allowing them to portray any emotion. Many newborn emotional expressions, such as anxiety, anger, and disgust, are not morphologically the same as emotions used by adults. These factors led to the development of the Baby Facial Action Coding System (Baby FACS), which is dedicated to the analysis of infants' Action Units (AU) and Emotional Facial Action Coding System (EMFACS).

Automatic facial expression recognition using these universal expressions could be a key component of natural human-machine interfaces, as well as in cognitive science and healthcare practice. Even though humans understand facial expressions almost instantly and without effort, reliable expression identification by machines remains a challenge. In that, Infant facial expression recognition is developing as a significant and technically demanding computer vision difficulty as compared to adult facial expressions recognition. The ability to accurately interpret infant facial expressions is important for the formation of professional parental care through surveillance footage analysis. Since there is a scarcity of infant facial expression data, the recognition is mostly based on the building of a dataset. There are no datasets publicly available or created particularly to analyze the expression of infants. The creation of a dataset for infant facial expression analysis is a big and challenging task. The ability to accurately interpret a baby's facial expressions is critical, as most of the expressions resemble the same. This process leads to the development of identifying the action behind the scenario. Despite recent advances in face detection, feature extraction procedures, and expression categorization approaches, designing an automated system that accomplishes this objective remains challenging.

This chapter provides an overview of the different datasets that are available for baby emotions. Additionally, it recommends the process for recognize newborn emotions through shot boundary detection, key frame extraction, Face detection algorithm, emotion classification through machine learning and deep learning approaches. The video sequence serves as input to the proposed methodology and is collected from a wide variety of available environments, including videos with known surroundings for infants and adults, cluttered background, stimulated situations, and videos with complex backgrounds. The video sequence is then separated into frames in order to retrieve key frames. From the retrieved key frames, faces are recognized using an integrated imaging technique and the identified faces are then divided into infants and adults using the CNN classifier model.

2. Available datasets

2.1 The city infant faces database

This database consists of 195 infant faces and it include 40 images of neutral infant faces, 54 images of negative infant faces, and 60 images of positive infant faces. High criterion validity and good test-retest reliability may be found in the images. There are 154 portrait images in the database, available in both color and black and white (**Figure 1**).

2.2 Babyexp

The dataset contains 5400 images depicting three different types of infant's face facial expressions: cry, laugh, and neutral. To appropriately describe additional universal facial expressions, these three expressions must first be recognized. For that process, initially, the images of infant actions such as crying and laughing are gathered from the private database named infant action database. The database contains footage of children performing various actions from which images of various actions have been taken. The images of neutral activity and some images of laughing were collected from the internet (**Figure 2**).

2.3 Rebel dataset

It comprises of 50 videos of infants aged 6–10 months that were gathered from the University of Nevada, Las Vegas' Department of Psychology (UNLV). There are a lot of unlabeled videos of infants in the Rebel collection that need to be labeled [2].

2.4 Tromso infant faces (TIF) database

In addition to rating the images' intensity, clarity, and valence, over 700 adult images divided them into 7 emotion categories: joyful, sad, disgusted, furious, terrified, astonished, and neutral.

2.5 The child emotion facial expression set

The seven induced and posed universal emotions as well as a neutral expression were utilized to build a video and image database of 4- to 6-year-old children.

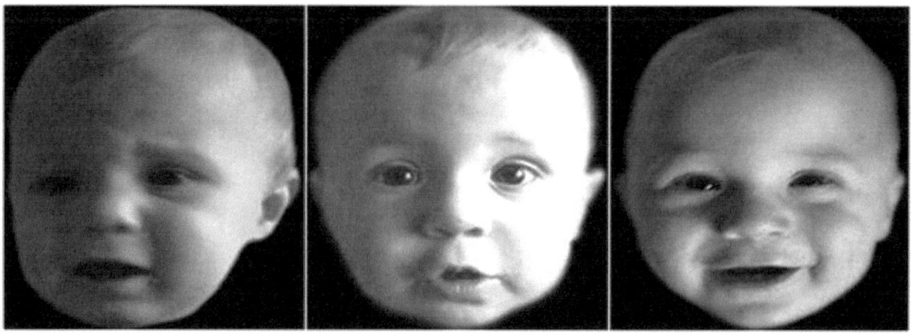

Figure 1.
Sample dataset images (city infant faces database) [1].

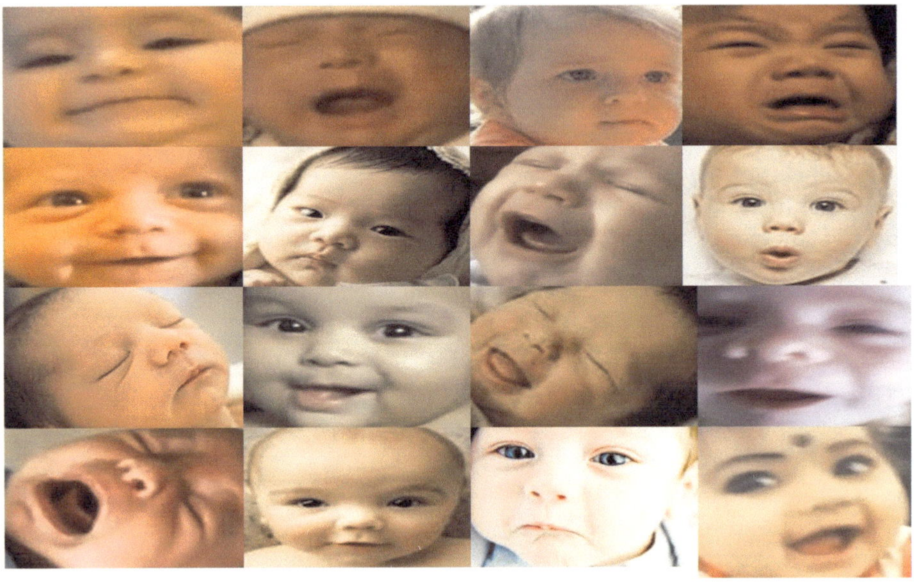

Figure 2.
Sample dataset images (Babyexp).

Participants were involved in video and image shoots intended to evoke certain emotions, and the resulting photos were then judged in two rounds by impartial judges. For each emotion, there were 87 stimuli for neutrality, 363 stimuli for joy, 170 stimuli for disgust, 104 stimuli for surprise, 152 stimuli for fear, 144 stimuli for sadness, 157 stimuli for anger, and 183 stimuli for contempt [3].

2.6 EmoReact

Children between the ages of 4 and 14 make up this multimodal emotion dataset. The collection includes 1102 audio-visual clips with annotations for 17 different emotional states, including 9 complicated emotions like frustration, doubt, and curiosity, as well as neutral and valence [4].

2.7 Child affective facial expression set (CAFE)

The CAFE collection includes 1192 color images of a racially and culturally varied group of children aged 2–8 who posed for six emotional facial expressions: angry, afraid, sad, joyful, astonished, and disgusted [5].

2.8 The multimodal dyadic behavior dataset

A solitary collection of multimodal (video, audio, and physiological) recordings of infants and toddlers' social and communicative behavior that was collected during a semi-structured play interaction with an adult. According to an IRB process endorsed by the university, the sessions were videotaped in the Georgia Tech Child Study Lab (CSL).

2.9 The NIMH Child Emotional Faces Picture Set (NIMH-ChEFS)

There are 482 images in the database of child faces in 2 different gaze states direct stare and averted gaze including those who are scared, angry, joyful, sad, and neutral [6].

3. Shot boundary detection method

A video is composed of a variety of scenes that capture the order of events, shots, and frames. As a result, it consists of interconnected images taken from various camera angles. The smallest unit of temporal visual information, a shot is composed of a series of related frames continuously recorded by a single camera. These time and space-related acts or events are represented by these frames [7]. In order to manage the immense volumes of video data created by massive multimedia applications, video abstraction technologies were required due to the rapid expansion of network infrastructure and the usage of advanced digital video technology. As a result, users may readily access and retrieve the necessary portions of the video without having to watch the whole thing. The key frame extraction module, where the number representative frames are recognized and chosen, and the shot boundary recognition module, which divides shots from video frames.

To streamline video analysis and processing, shot boundary detection/temporal video segmentation is the technique of dividing video frames into several shots by identifying the border between subsequent video shots. The primary objective of shot boundary detection methods is to identify differences in visual content. These differences between succeeding images are calculated, and a threshold comparison is formed. Three fundamental components make up the shot boundary detection (SBD) method algorithms: frame representation, dissimilarity measure, and thresholding. Finding transitions in the context of abrupt illumination changes and significant camera/object movement is one of these SBD approaches' biggest challenges, which might result in the extraction of incorrect keyframes.

4. Key frame extraction

Based on shot boundary, visual information, movement analysis, and cluster approach, key frame extraction techniques may be loosely divided into four categories. By removing or deleting the duplicated frames from the source film and extracting a group of representative frames, keyframe extraction is an appropriate technique for communicating effectively the key components of a video clip. These removed keyframes are anticipated to represent and offer thorough visual data for the entire video [8]. To make indexing, retrieval, storage management, and video data recognition more convenient and effective, the keyframe technique is used to reduce the computational cost and amount of data required for video processing. These approaches can be classified into three main classes viz., shot based, sampling-based, and clustering-based techniques.

4.1 Sampling-based technique

This sort of technique, which does not prioritize the video content, chooses representative frames by equally or randomly sampling the video frames from the original video. The idea behind this method is to select every *k*th frame from the source video [9]. The length of the video determines this value of *k*. A typical range for a video summary is 5–15% of the entire video. Every 20th frame is chosen as the keyframe in the case of 5% summarizing, whereas every 7th frame is chosen in the case of 15% summarization. Although these keyframes were extracted from the video, they do not accurately depict everything. They can also result in duplicate frames with the same content.

4.2 Shot-based technique

In this method, the shot boundary/transition is initially detected using an effective SBD method. The keyframe extraction method is then carried out after the video frames have been divided into multiple shots. Different key frame selection methods have been covered in various literary categories. The first and last frames of the candidate shot are often chosen as the key frames in the conventional method. These snipped key frames are the shots' representative frames, which results in a more simplified synopsis of the original video.

4.3 Clustering-based technique

Unsupervised learning techniques such as clustering group together collections of related data points. With this technique, video file frames with comparable visual contents are divided into various numbers of clusters. The frame that is extracted as the key frame from each cluster is the one that is closest to the candidate cluster's center. The qualities that the frames display, such as color histograms, texture, saliency maps, and motion, define the similarities between them [10]. The fundamental problem with the clustering-based approach is that, before completing the clustering operation, it can be challenging to count the number of clusters in each video file.

5. Face detection algorithm

Object detection is one of the computer technologies that is connected to image processing and computer vision. It is concerned with detecting instances of an object such as human faces, buildings, trees, cars, etc. The primary aim of face detection algorithms is to determine whether there is any face in an image or not.

- Viola-Jones: In order to find Haar-like characteristics, this method slides a square of a predefined size across the image. Then, these characteristics can be identified as components of a face.

- One-shot detector (SSD): This one overlays the image with a grid and many "anchor boxes," the latter of which are produced during the training phase. These boxes are used to identify the necessary items' characteristics and locations, such as faces.

- You Only Have to Look Once (YOLO): Because it just takes one "look" at the image to detect all the objects of interest, it boasts better performance than SSD. only needs one "look" at the picture to find all the objects of interest.

6. Classification methods

6.1 Machine learning

Automatic facial expressions classifiers have made significant progress, according to researchers. Facial Action Coding System (FACS) has been developed for classifying facial movements by AU [11]. Traditional machine learning-based classifiers such as Hidden Markov Model, Support Vector Machine (SVM), Bayesian network were proposed for face facial expressions recognition. Audio and video clips are used to recognize and classify emotions by SVM and Decision Level Fusion [12]. Utilizing the compound emotion recognition of children experiencing meltdown crises, a preventive strategy was developed and implemented. Unusual facial expressions linked to complex emotions are clearly connected to the symptoms of meltdowns. Experimental evaluation is done on several deep spatiotemporal geometric features of autistic children's micro expressions during a meltdown. To choose the qualities that most clearly distinguish compound emotion in a meltdown crisis in autistic children from compound emotion in a normal state, Compound Emotion Recognition performance and several collections of micro expressions features are compared. For learning and categorizing the features extracted from many images, the nearest neighbor method was introduced.

6.2 Deep learning

Deep learning-based face expression detection has gained popularity as a result of the growth of huge data and computer efficiency. YOLOv3-tiny is used to detect the face and body of infants, and it has a classification accuracy of 94.46% for the face and 86.53% for the body of infants. For extracting local temporal and spatial features, a two-stream CNNs model is used. Models based on transfer learning, including VGG16, Resnet 18, and 50, have been suggested for recognizing adult facial emotions [13–15]. In order to distinguish the newborn's facial emotions from images, a deep neural network must be built since infant facial expression recognition is necessary in parenting care. The transfer learning model-based techniques suffer from overfitting since there is a dearth of data on newborn facial expressions. Based on IOT edge computing and a multi-headed 1-dimensional convolutional neural network (1D-CNN), a real-time infant facial expression detection system. It was suggested to use face recognition and emotion recognition algorithms to monitor toddlers' emotions. To lower the number of parameters and save computational resources, this suggests a lightweight network structure constructed using the deep learning approach. A methodology for AI-based facial emotion recognition that uses many datasets, feature extraction methods, and algorithms. The datasets are broken down into three groups: children, adults, and senior citizens in order to better understand the vast application of facial expression identification. Modern CNN models are utilized for preprocessing, feature extraction, and classification while using a variety of techniques. Additionally, it evaluates the benchmark accuracy of various CNN models as well as some architectural traits.

7. Shallow CNN architecture

An eleven-layer shallow convolutional neural network was developed to recognize newborn facial expressions. The suggested shallow network architecture is

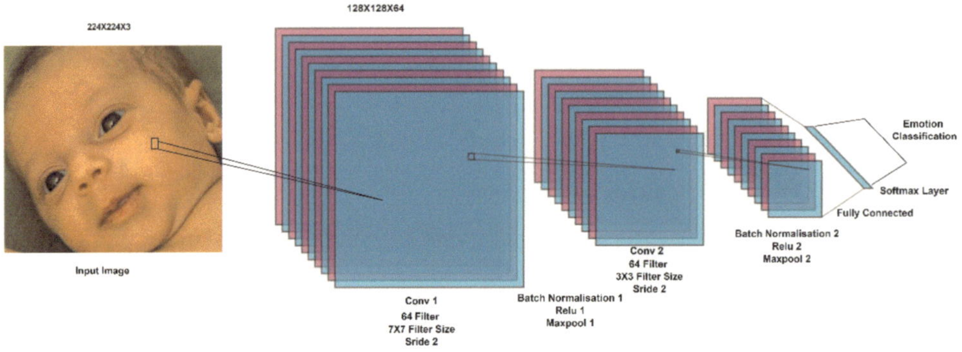

Figure 3.
The proposed shallow CNN model [16].

shown in **Figure 3**. The network is composed of two groups of convolutional layers, two maxpool layers, a fully connected layer, a SoftMax layer, and a layer for classification output. One convolution layer, batch normalization, and the relu activation function are all present in the group. The input layer is fixed to be 224 × 224 × 3 with zero center normalization. Following that, 64 filters with a 7 × 7 grid size are convolved with the input layer. Batch normalization of the convolution filter output is done for independent learning, and then a relu activation layer is applied to provide linearity.

Following that, the maxpool operation is used to extract the low-level characteristics. This prevents hazy problems and draws attention to the key details of an infant image. The features are once more convolved with 64 3 × 3 sized filters, 64 batch normalized filters, an activation function, and a maxpool layer. The representation of features is enhanced and the learning parameters are decreased by this structure. The completely linked layer, a SoftMax, and the classification output layer are attached to the structure's end.

7.1 Training

In order to maintain a constant image size, the data is initially supplemented throughout the training phase. The learning rate, which is inversely proportional to the gradient descent, is one of the most significant adjustments hyperparameters. Dynamic learning rate adjustment has been employed to get the best feature learning of the infant's facial expressions. For that, the initial learning rate is set at 0.01, and the learning rate is multiplied by 0.1 after every 100 iterations. In order to prevent overfitting, a simple and generalized architecture with stochastic gradient descent and momentum has been developed. It is ideally suited for the new infant images. The best training model is chosen after the model has undergone several modifications.

7.2 Testing

The model is trained and tested using MATLAB 2021b with a GPU processor. The dataset primarily includes the three newborn facial expressions of scream, laugh, and neutral, as seen in **Figure 4**. Each infant has a different set of facial expressions. However, they do possess a few defining characteristics that make identification difficult. There are roughly 1800 photos in each class. Resizing is one of the data

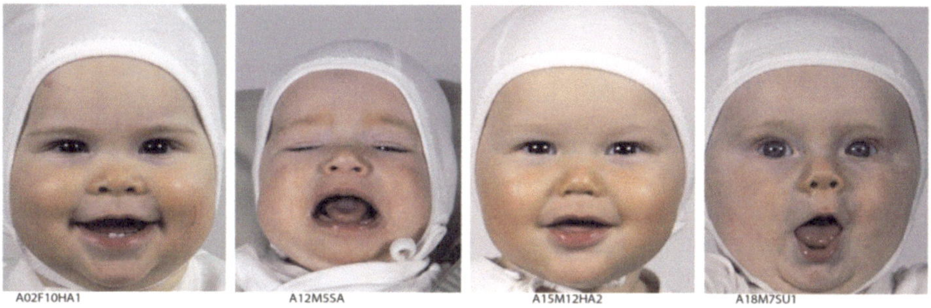

Figure 4.
Sample dataset images (TIF) [17].

augmentation techniques used to equalise the size distribution because the photos collected in the dataset and on the website are of different sizes. This method increases the diversity and adaptability of the model. Along with validation and testing accuracy, the review process currently includes precision and recall and it is depicted in Eqs. (1), (2) and (3)

$$\text{Accuracy} = \frac{(\text{True Positive} + \text{True Negative})}{(\text{True Positive} + \text{False Positive} + \text{True Negative} + \text{False Negative})} \tag{1}$$

$$\text{Precision} = \frac{\text{True Positive}}{(\text{True Positivee} + \text{False Positive})} \tag{2}$$

$$\text{Recall} = \frac{\text{True Positive}}{(\text{True Positivee} + \text{False Negative})} \tag{3}$$

Resnet 18, Resnet 50, and VGG 16 are the traditional and benchmark facial expression recognition networks. These are more sophisticated network models that employ complicated elements to deliver the best outcomes for facial expression recognition. As a result, this study compares different topologies to the suggested shallow network. **Table 1** displays the suggested shallow network's architectures with Resnet 50 and VGG 16.

The suggested shallow network's input picture has a size of 224 × 224 pixels. 64 stride 2 and 7 × 7 convolution kernels are used in the Conv1 layer's filters. The output size is consequently decreased to 112 112 pixels. The next step is to establish a batch normalization with the same scale, offset, relu activation layer, and max pool layer. The same set of Conv2 layers is created with only a 3 × 3 change in the convolution layer kernel size. This shrinks the output to a 56 × 56 size. To determine the type of infant facial expressions, a fully connected layer with three categories and a classification layer is implemented.

The overall design process contributes in stabilizing learning and significantly reduces the quantity of epochs required to train the networks. It avoids the exponential growth of the compute needed to learn the network. Other networks require more time to execute and train since they are spatially more complicated. The suggested network has a less complex structural level than the other networks in **Table 1**. By using less hardware resources, it also saves time and makes the training process less challenging. The proposed approach is therefore more computationally effective and

Layer name	Resnet-18	Resnet-50	VGG-16	Shallow CNN
Conv1	7 × 7, 64, stride 2	7 × 7,64, stride 2	3 × 3 max pool, stride 2 $\begin{bmatrix} 3\times3, 64 \\ 3\times3, 64 \end{bmatrix} \times 2$	7 × 7, 64, stride 2 Batch normalization, Relu, 3 × 3 max pool, stride 2
Conv2	3 × 3 maxpool, stride 2 $\begin{bmatrix} 3\times3, 64 \\ 3\times3, 64 \end{bmatrix} \times 2$	3 × 3 max pool, stride 2 $\begin{bmatrix} 1\times1, 64 \\ 3\times3, 64 \\ 1\times1,256 \end{bmatrix} \times 3$	3 × 3 max pool, stride 2 $\begin{bmatrix} 3\times3,128 \\ 3\times3,128 \end{bmatrix} \times 2$	3 × 3, 64, stride 2 Batch normalization, Relu, 3 × 3 max pool, stride 2
Conv3	$\begin{bmatrix} 3\times3,128 \\ 3\times3,128 \end{bmatrix} \times 2$	$\begin{bmatrix} 1\times1,128 \\ 3\times3,128 \\ 1\times1,512 \end{bmatrix} \times 3$	3 × 3 max pool, stride 2 $\begin{bmatrix} 3\ 3,256 \\ 3\times3,256 \\ 3\times3,256 \end{bmatrix} \times 3$	—
Conv4	$\begin{bmatrix} 3\times3,256 \\ 3\times3,256 \end{bmatrix} \times 2$	$\begin{bmatrix} 1\times1,256 \\ 3\times3,256 \\ 1\times1, 1024 \end{bmatrix} \times 3$	3 × 3 max pool, stride 2 $\begin{bmatrix} 3x3,512 \\ 3x3,512 \\ 3x3,512 \end{bmatrix} \times 3$	—
Conv5	$\begin{bmatrix} 3\times3,512 \\ 3\times3,512 \end{bmatrix} \times 2$	$\begin{bmatrix} 1\times1,512 \\ 3\times3,512 \\ 1\times1, 2048 \end{bmatrix} \times 3$	3 × 3 max pool, stride 2 $\begin{bmatrix} 3\times3,512 \\ 3\times3,512 \\ 3\times3,512 \end{bmatrix} \times 3$	—
	Average pool, 1000-d fc	Average pool, 1000-d fc	fc with 4096 nodes	—
	6-d fc,softmax	6-d fc,softmax	fc with 4096 nodes, softmax with 1000 nods	3-dfc, softmax, classification

Table 1.
Architectures of ResNet-18, ResNet-50, VGG16, and the proposed shallow CNN.

yields better performance results. The Pareto principle is utilized to divide the dataset's photos, with 15% of the images being used for validation and 70% being used for training. The remaining 15% is used only for testing. Thus, 1260 images are selected for training, 270 for validation, and 270 for testing out of a total of 1800 images. The suggested method's training curve, depicted in **Figure 5**, comprises data on the loss curve as well as training and validation accuracy.

The experiments have been conducted using a local dataset that had been trained and validated using current techniques (**Table 2**). In general, the learning capacity grows along with the number of layers. However, overfitting difficulties could occur if the learning capacity is sufficiently large. It will perform incredibly well during training but poorly during testing. Performance of the proposed network is contrasted with that of the current network, as shown in **Table 3**. It demonstrates that the suggested strategy produces improved accuracy. The accuracy, precision and recall are calculated the values (True Positive, True Negative, False Positive, False Negative) taken from confusion matrix. For example, when the accuracy of 1260 samples is calculated, the proposed model gets True Positive of 1136 and True Negative of 94, and it obtained an average training accuracy of 97.16%.

On the local dataset and the BabyExp dataset, respectively, are used to operate the suggested network's outcomes. **Table 3** compares these two networks and demonstrates that the suggested approach performs better. The suggested approach is shallow in comparison to VEFSO-DLSE [18], CNN gets a better average accuracy result of

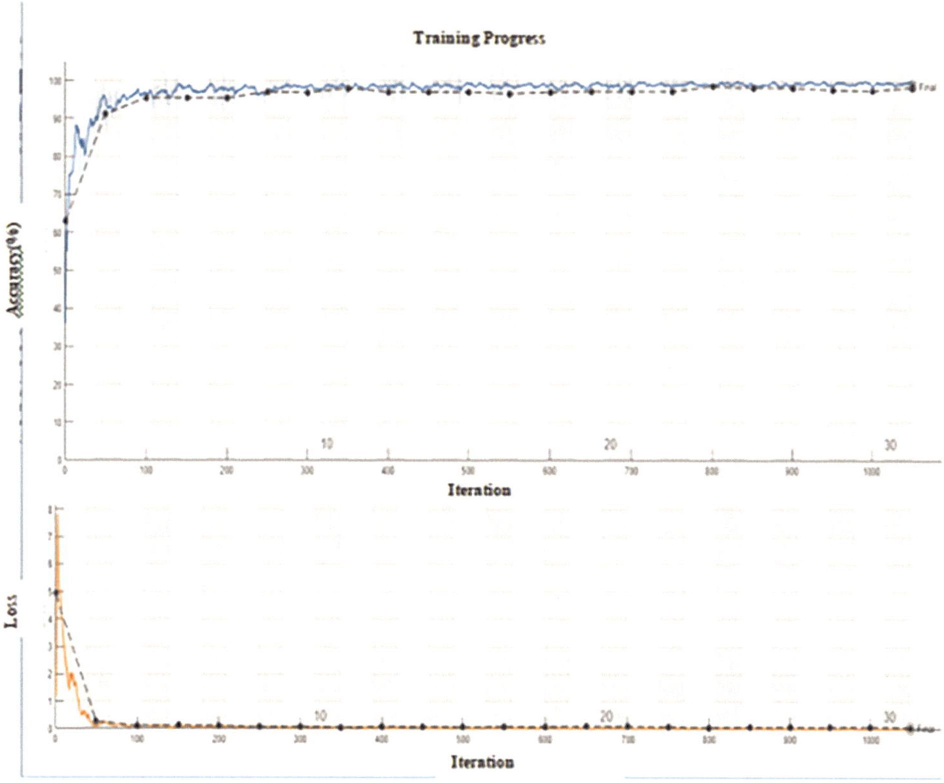

Figure 5.
Training and validation curve.

	Laugh		Cry		Neutral		Overall
	Precision	**Recall**	**Precision**	**Recall**	**Precision**	**Recall**	**Average accuracy**
VFESO-DLSE [18]	93.18	78.5	85.07	96.27	86.71	88.86	93.6
Shallow CNN	**97.8**	**98**	**96**	**97.2**	**98**	**97.8**	**97.4**
Shallow CNN (10 fold validation)	**95.6**	**96.4**	**95.3**	**96.8**	**97**	**96.2**	**96.21**

Table 2.
Performance comparison (pretrained CNN vs. proposed shallow CNN).

97.4% and a cross-validation accuracy of 96.21%. The computational advantage of the proposed method achieves through the compact in size with the floating point operations per second of 1.54M. The experimental finding demonstrates that the proposed strategy extracts more useful features than alternative approaches. Similar relationships between actual and anticipated facial expressions are demonstrated by other models. The matrix shows that certain neutral photos are incorrectly grouped with other images. The similarity between the images, which can be seen by examining them, increases the complexity. The suggested approach, however, produces greater accuracy while avoiding the overfitting issue.

	Laugh		Cry		Neutral		Overall	
	Precision	**Recall**	**Precision**	**Recall**	**Precision**	**Recall**	**Testing accuracy**	**Average accuracy**
Resnet-18	91.21	94.7	93	92.7	89	93.2	96	94
Resnet-50	94.3	95.6	91.74	90.6	94.3	95.6	92.6	90.26
VGG-16	92.1	94	89.91	90.3	94.26	94	95	93.6
Shallow CNN	**97.8**	**98**	**96**	**97.2**	**98**	**97.8**	**97.8**	**97.4**

Table 3.
Performance comparison of proposed method vs. VFESO-DLSE [18].

8. Conclusion

In the field of computer vision, the ability to recognize baby emotion is significant as it provides prognostic data for diagnosing ADHD and ASD. This chapter outlines the methods for identifying and preventing these conditions in the earlier stage. It also provides empirical support for infant development by learning subtle information from their faces. Infant facial expression recognition study raises some significant issues, such as the transfer learning model's decreased learning capacity and the recognition system's low stability. A thorough framework for early medical condition diagnosis and parental oversight using machine learning and deep learning techniques is presented in this chapter. The suggested network resolves these problems by recommending a two-stage model with a shallow neural network to save space. The minimal quantity of data generated from the videos and obtained from the websites is used in the suggested shallow network model. With 97.8% accuracy throughout testing, this model performs well. It also needs less time to train because it has the ideal learning capacity. Therefore, the suggested chapter offers superior intelligent interpersonal interactions and is well suited to the field of parental surveillance and care.

Author details

Uma Maheswari Pandyan[1]*, Mohamed Mansoor Roomi Sindha[2], Priya Kannapiran[2], Senthilarasi Marimuthu[2] and Vinora Anbunathan[1]

1 Velammal College of Engineering and Technology, Madurai, Tamil Nadu, India

2 Thiagarajar College of Engineering, Madurai, Tamil Nadu, India

*Address all correspondence to: umamahes.p@gmail.com

References

[1] Webb R, Ayers S, Endress A. The city infant faces database: a validated set of infant facial expressions. Behavior Research Methods. 2018;**50**(1): 151-159. DOI: 10.3758/s13428-017-0859-9. PMID: 28205132; PMCID: PMC5809537

[2] Huguet Cabot P-L, Navigli R. REBEL: Relation Extraction By End-to-end Language generation, 2021, Findings of the Association for Computational Linguistics: EMNLP. 2021

[3] Gioia NJ, Alexandra Caldas OA, Rinaldo Focaccia S, Renne Gerber LV, Elisa Harumi L, D'Antino MEF. The child emotion facial expression set: A database for emotion recognition in children. Frontiers in Psychology. 2021; **12**:1664-1078. Available from: https://www.frontiersin.org/articles/10.3389/fpsyg. 2021.666245

[4] Nojavanasghari B, Baltrušaitis T, Hughes C, Morency L-P. Emoreact: A Multimodal Approach and Dataset for Recognizing Emotional Responses in Children. In: Proceedings of the ACM International Conference on Multimodal Interaction (ICMI). 2016

[5] Vanessa L, Cat T. The Child Affective Facial Expression (CAFE) set: validity and reliability from untrained adults. Frontiers in Psychology. 2015;**5**: 1664-1078. Available from: https://www.frontiersin.org/articles/10.3389/fpsyg. 2014.01532

[6] Egger HL, Pine DS, Nelson E, Leibenluft E, Ernst M, Towbin KE, Angold A. The NIMH Child Emotional Faces Picture Set (NIMH-ChEFS): a new set of children's facial emotion stimuli. International Journal of Methods in Psychiatric Research. 2011;**20**(3): 145-156. DOI: 10.1002/mpr.343. PMID: 22547297; PMCID: PMC3342041

[7] Chakraborty S, Thounaojam DM, Sinha N. A shot boundary detection technique based on visual colour information. Multimedia Tools and Applications. 2021;**80**:4007-4022. DOI: 10.1007/s11042-020-09857-8

[8] Sheena CV, Narayanan NK. Key-frame extraction by analysis of histograms of video frames using statistical methods. Procedia Computer Science. 2015;**70**:36-40. ISSN 18770509. DOI: 10.1016/j.procs.2015.10.021

[9] Kingston Z, Moll M, Kavraki LE. Sampling-based methods for motion planning with constraints. Annual Review of Control, Robotics, and Autonomous Systems. 2018;**1**:159-185

[10] Ming Z, Bugeau A, Rouas J, Shochi T. Facial action units intensity estimation by the fusion of features with multi-kernel Support Vector Machine. In: 2015 11th IEEE International Conference and Workshops on Automatic Face and Gesture Recognition (FG). 2015. pp. 1-6

[11] Lee Y, Kim KK, Kim JH. Prevention of Safety Accidents through Artificial Intelligence Monitoring of Infants in the Home Environment. In: International Conference on Information and Communication Technology Convergence ICTC). 2019. pp. 474-477

[12] Li B, Lima D. Facial expression recognition via ResNet-50. International Journal of Cognitive Computing in Engineering. 2021;**2**:57-64. ISSN 2666-3074

[13] Altamura M, Padalino FA, Stella E. Facial emotion recognition in bipolar

disorder and healthy aging. Journal of Nervous and Mental Disease. 2016; **204**(3):188-193

[14] Majumder A, Behera L, Subramanian V. Automatic facial expression recognition system using deep network-based data fusion. IEEE Transactions on Cybernetics. 2016:1-12. DOI: 10.1109/TCYB.2016.2625419

[15] Lin Q, He R, Jiang P. Feature Guided CNN for Baby's Facial Expression Recognition. 2020. Article ID 8855885. DOI: 10.1155/2020/8855885

[16] Uma Maheswari P, Mohamed Mansoor Roomi S, Senthilarasi M, Priya K, Shankar Mahadevan G. Shallow CNN Model for Recognition of Infants Facial Expression. In: 4th International Conference on Machine Intelligence and Signal Processing, MISP. 2022

[17] Maack JK, Bohne A, Nordahl D, Livsdatter L, Lindahl AAW, Overvoll M, et al. The Tromso Infant Faces Database (TIF): development, validation and application to assess parenting experience on clarity and intensity ratings. Frontiers in Psychology. 2017. Sec. Quantitative Psychology and Measurement. DOI: 10.3389/fpsyg.2017.00409

[18] Lin Q, He R, Jiang P. Feature Guided CNN for Baby's Facial Expression Recognition, Complexity, Hindawi, Volume 2020, Article ID 8855885, 10. pp. 2020

Chapter 4

Facial Emotion Recognition Feature Extraction: A Survey

Michele Mukeshimana, Abraham Niyongere and Jérémie Ndikumagenge

Abstract

Facial emotion recognition is a process based on facial expression to automatically recognize individual emotion expression. Automatic recognition refers to creating computer systems that are able to simulate human natural ability of detection, analysis, and determination of emotion by facial expression. Human natural recognition uses various points of observation to make decision or conclusion on emotion expressed by the present person in front. Facial features efficiently extracted aid in improving the classifier performance and application efficiency. Many feature extraction methods based on shape, texture, and other local features are proposed in the literature, and this chapter will review them. This chapter will survey some recent and formal feature expression methods from video and image products and classify them according to their efficiency and application.

Keywords: facial emotion recognition (FER), feature extraction, human computer interaction, automatic emotion recognition, machine learning

1. Introduction

Recent research in Computer Science is more driven by constructing a solution smarter product (hardware and software). Computing is becoming ubiquitous and pervasive, with human at the center. Devices are attaining more ability to average human intelligent actions and interactions. Human beings are basically emotional and affective. They express their emotion in many ways and they require emotion expression in their natural interaction no matter what they interact with (human, machine, or nature) [1]. Together with the objective of having human-centered digital solutions, affective computing aims to endow computers with the ability of sensing, recognition, and expressing emotion [2, 3].

Automatic emotion recognition is one of the recent research trends in Artificial Intelligence, especially in the field of Machine Learning. Based on scientific ground, emotion recognition is about a mapping from feature space to emotion descriptors or label space. This feature space is built from different identified cues extracted from an original element, which is the subject of study [4]. These cues seem to help distinguish two different situations or cases during a classification task and minimize differences within elements of the same class.

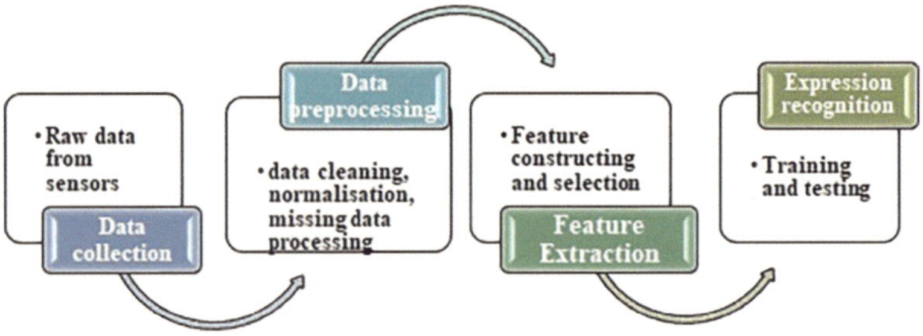

Figure 1.
Emotion recognition processes.

In order to recognize human affect state automatically, some of the steps studied and worked on consist of data collection, data preprocessing, feature extraction, and emotion recognition, as represented in **Figure 1**.

Data collection as the first step in automatic recognition consists of reassembling raw data from different sensors according to the work at hand, that is, the modality to study or its application [5]. This chapter is about acquiring a video with a recognizable human face and expressing emotion. Collected data are tarnished with many noises and unwanted details that need to be removed [6, 7]. Data preprocessing generally involves data cleaning, normalization (or standardization), and missing data processing. Cleaned data serve as basic space for extraction of main features, which convey more information for an expected pattern. The feature extraction step consists of representing data in a digital form to present to a filter. It draws out the values, which are more informative and nonredundant for a future easy learning process and quick generalization.

It is very important to extract an effective facial representation from all considered facial images for any effective facial expression recognition system. The resulting representation should preserve indispensable information possessing distinguished contrast power and stability, which lessens within-class variations of expressions whereas expands between-class variations [8]. Extracted features aid in emotion classification [9]. At this level, two procedures are done: training a classifier and testing it. Emotion classification is the last step, resulting in the process of classification of a new case into its category using the trained classifier. Classification performance is greatly subjective to the quality of information contained in the expression representations [10]. Thus, the step of feature extraction has a great influence on the classification outcome.

This chapter contains a global point of view on feature extraction, and different types of facial expression recognition feature extraction methods are detailed in the following chapters.

2. Feature extraction

Features are also called attributes or input variables. Feature extraction consists in draw out the feature relating to the modality. The precision of the most relevant feature for extraction in emotion recognition research is still an open topic [11–13]. However, the often-studied modalities are face expression, speech, body motion, hand gestures, and physiological signals. They are the representation of the data and can be in binary form, categorical, discrete, or continuous. Feature extraction is subdivided into two processes, that is, features construction and feature selection.

2.1 Feature construction

The feature construction consists of determining the good data representation, according to the domain specifications and measurements availability [13]. The extracted features are proper to modalities and an interesting task. In emotion recognition, feature extraction focuses on cues that convey better the affect expression. Actually, referring to human natural emotion or intention expression and perception, there are many studies that have proved some frequently observed units to convey useful information for emotion categorization.

Table 1 represents a summary of the frequently observed and studied units for feature extraction, according to the recording methods or the study of interest.

Table 1 presents a summary of the list of the combinations and cues considered according to modality in the study. Modality means any human body parts that can be used to express emotion. In affect detection, some basic units encompass other intermediate units. This list relates to the most cited elements in the literature. The modalities are defined as the main objectively observed entities, which convey most information about emotion expression. Basic units are the small elements of the whole modality and can stand for an independent study [14–18]. Intermediate units are more detailed than the basic units. These unity measurements produce multiple feature values, which constitute the vector feature of the modality [19]. The features

Modality		**Units**	
		Basic	**Intermediates**
Face expression		Eyes, eyebrows, nose, mouth	Action Units, pupil
Speech		Linguistic	Word, multi-word, phrases, sentences, documents
		Paralinguistic	Pitch intensity of utterances, bandwidth, duration, voice quality, Mel frequency Cepstral coefficients (MFCC)
Body	Head gestures	Head position	
		Head movement	
	Hand Gestures	Shape	
		Motion; keystrokes	
	Body motion	Spinal column	Neck, chest and abdomen
		DOF body	Symmetrical arms
		Body center mass	Movement of body center of mass
		Joints	Degree of joint rotation
Physiologic		Hearth Brain Limbs Blood	Electrocardiogram (ECG); breath rate; electro-dermal activity (EDA); electro-myogram (EMG)

Table 1.
Modality and extracted features.

Toolkit	Modality	Feature extracted/functionality	Brief description
PRAAT [22]	Audio	Duration, F0, Range, Movement, Slope, Energy features	PRAAT (a system for doing phonetics)
FEELTRACE [23, 24]	Audio	Labeling	Allowing the emotional dynamics of speech episodes to be examined.
OpenEAR [25]	Audio	Signal Energy, Loudness, Mel-/ Bark-/Octave-Spectra, MFCC, PLP-CC	openEAR provides efficient (audio) feature extraction.
OpenSMILE [26]	Audio	Signal Energy, Loudness, Formants, Mel-/ Bark-/Octave-Spectra, MFCC, PLP-CC, Pitch, Voice quality (Jitter, Shimmer), LPC, Line Spectral, Pairs(LSP), Spectral, Shape description	It is an open source toolkit, for feature extraction in machine learning and data mining [27]
EyesWeb [28]	Body	Quantity of motion, cue, Contraction index of the body, velocity, Acceleration, fluidity of the hand's, barycenter	Open software for extended Multimodal Interaction.
Luxand FSDK 1.7	Face	Action units	Facial recognition software [29]
ANVIL [30]	Audio	Annotation tool in a multimodal dialog	Free for research purposes [31]

Table 2.
Some automatic feature extraction tools.

construction can be manually processed and/or complemented by automatic feature construction methods [20, 21].

Recently, the research in feature extraction techniques has ended up by proposing some automatic feature extraction tools and algorithms. Some examples are given in **Table 2**.

In **Table 2**, the toolkit column corresponds to the name given to the tool or algorithm in the literature. The modality column means the channel conveying needed information. The listed tools are mostly available online and free of charge, and are compatible with the most popular platforms, such as Windows, Linux, and Macintosh. The references within the table are the work that has utilized the tool or the reports of the authors.

The step of feature construction builds a feature set which is full of some unnecessary or superfluous data. In order to clean that feature set, a feature selection is necessary to prepare a proper dataset useful in the learning process.

2.2 Feature selection

The step of features selection mainly aims to select some features, which are more relevant and explanatory to the study in view. The feature construction creates thousands of features that require an important amount of storage and slows down the training process, the curse of dimensionality. The feature selection uses a data reduction method to eliminate irrelevant and redundant information to a sufficient minimum dimension. The main objective is to get attributes with a large distance between classes and small variance in the same class [7].

The step of feature extraction success affects the training process, recognition accuracy, and application efficiency. It constitutes a subject of study on its own, and it is the subject of the present work, extensions are limited to facial feature extraction.

3. Facial expression feature extraction

Facial feature extraction is all about exactly localizing different features on the face, which include the detection of eyes, brows, mouth, nose, chin, etc. [32]. Facial features are often subdivided into appearance or transient features and geometric or intransient features [10, 33, 34]. Local appearance-based methods extract appearance changes of the face or a region of the face, while geometric features express the shape of the facial components (eyebrows, eyes, mouth, etc.) and the location of prominent points of the face (comers of the eyes, mouth, etc.).

3.1 Geometric feature extraction

3.1.1 Facial feature points (FFP)

The shape and location-related features could be achieved using Active Appearance Methods (AAM) [35]. It has been used to label 68 facial feature points (FFPs) as related in the work of Wu et al. [36]. Facial feature points are visible marks in facial images or points that constitute interesting part of images, such as eye centers, nose tip, mouth corners, and other salient facial points. They are often used as a reference or for measurement. **Figure 2** represents an example of the FFPs extracted based on the AAM alignment and the corresponding animation parameters, and this figure is extracted from the work of Wu et al. [36].

Facial feature points are also referred to as facial points, fiducial facial points, or facial landmarks [37]. The points shown in **Figure 2** can be concatenated to represent a shape $x = (x_1, \cdots, x_N, y_1, \cdots, y_N)^T$, where (x_i, y_i) denotes the location of the i-th point and N is the number of points (here **Figure 2**, N equals 68). The FFPs are grouped into Facial Animation Parameters (FAPs), to facilitate the normalization among people. Every FAP limits a segment of a key distance on the face. The AAM was initially developed in the work of Cootes and Taylor [35], and has presented strong promise in multiple technologies of facial recognition technologies, including in recognizing emotions by its ability to both aid in beginning face-search algorithms and feature extraction based on texture and shape [38].

Extracted facial feature points (FFPs)

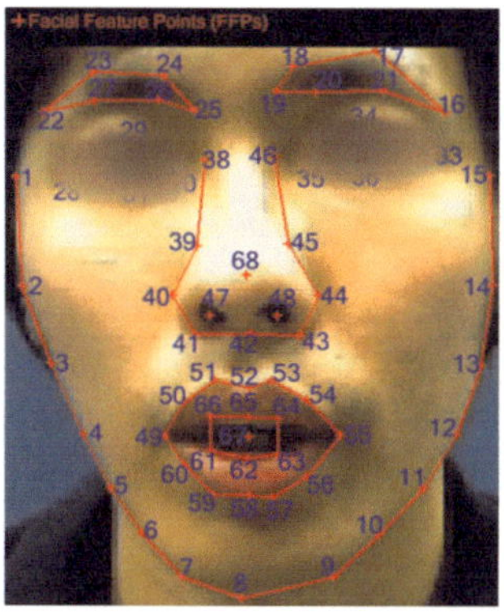

Facial regions	FAPs Num.	Euclidean distance between FFPs	Comparing FFPs displacement with neutral frame
Eyebrows	1, 2	$D_{vertical,1}(22, 30)$, $D_{vertical,2}(16, 35)$	$D_{v,1\_Neutral}$-$D_{v,1}$, $D_{v,2\_Neutral}$-$D_{v,2}$
	3, 4	$D_{vertical,3}(25, 30)$, $D_{vertical,4}(19, 35)$	$D_{v,3\_Neutral}$-$D_{v,3}$, $D_{v,4\_Neutral}$-$D_{v,4}$
	5, 6	$D_{vertical,5}(22, 28)$, $D_{vertical,6}(16, 33)$	$D_{v,5\_Neutral}$-$D_{v,5}$, $D_{v,6\_Neutral}$-$D_{v,6}$
	7, 8	$D_{vertical,7}(23, 28)$, $D_{vertical,8}(17, 33)$	$D_{v,7\_Neutral}$-$D_{v,7}$, $D_{v,8\_Neutral}$-$D_{v,8}$
	9, 10	$D_{vertical,9}(25, 28)$, $D_{vertical,10}(19, 33)$	$D_{v,9\_Neutral}$-$D_{v,9}$, $D_{v,10\_Neutral}$-$D_{v,10}$
	11, 12	$D_{vertical,11}(23, 30)$, $D_{vertical,12}(17, 35)$	$D_{v,11\_Neutral}$-$D_{v,11}$, $D_{v,12\_Neutral}$-$D_{v,12}$
	13	$D_{m,13}(19, 25)$	$D_{h,13\_Neutral}$-$D_{h,13}$
Eyes	14, 15	$D_{vertical,14}(29, 31)$, $D_{vertical,15}(34, 36)$	$D_{v,14\_Neutral}$-$D_{v,14}$, $D_{v,15\_Neutral}$-$D_{v,15}$
	16, 17	$D_{vertical,16}(28, 49)$,$D_{vertical,17}(33, 55)$	$D_{v,16\_Neutral}$-$D_{v,16}$, $D_{v,17\_Neutral}$-$D_{v,17}$
	18, 19	$D_{horizontal,18}(28, 30)$,$D_{horizontal,19}(33, 35)$	$D_{h,1\_18Neutral}$-$D_{h,18}$, $D_{h,19\_Neutral}$-$D_{h,19}$
Nose	20, 21	$D_{vertical,20}(52, 68)$, $D_{vertical,21}(58, 68)$	$D_{v,20\_Neutral}$-$D_{v,20}$, $D_{v,21\_Neutral}$-$D_{v,21}$
	22, 23	$D_{vertical,22}(49, 68)$, $D_{vertical,23}(55, 68)$	$D_{v,22\_Neutral}$-$D_{v,22}$, $D_{v,23\_Neutral}$-$D_{v,23}$
Mouth	24, 25	$D_{vertical,24}(52, 58)$, $D_{horizontal,25}(49, 55)$	$D_{v,24\_Neutral}$-$D_{v,24}$, $D_{h,25\_Neutral}$-$D_{h,25}$
Facial Contours	26, 27	$D_{horizontal,26}(5, 58)$, $D_{horizontal,27}(11, 58)$	$D_{h,26\_Neutral}$-$D_{h,26}$, $D_{h,27\_Neutral}$-$D_{h,27}$
	28, 29	$D_{horizontal,28}(2, 68)$, $D_{horizontal,29}(14, 68)$	$D_{h,28\_Neutral}$-$D_{h,28}$, $D_{h,29\_Neutral}$-$D_{h,29}$
	30	$D_{vertical,30}(8, 68)$	$D_{v,30\_Neutral}$-$D_{v,30}$

Figure 2.
Example of facial feature points labeled using AAM alignment [36].

3.1.2 Facial affective coding systems (FACS)

Other works consider the Facial Affective Coding System (FACS) and define the Active Unities (AUs) as the facial muscle action [39, 40]. Facial action unit research studies the movement of facial muscles [41] and describes facial movement changes. Based on the work of Ekman Paul and Friesen [42], Facial Action Coding System (FACS) contributes as one of the most representative methods for facial expression application in measurement technology. Action units can precisely extract facial expressions, but they are less applied in facial expression recognition because of their exact positioning. **Figure 3** represents some examples of Action Unities.

In **Figure 3**, the examples display the considered action unities detected on facial images. Those action units are randomly chosen for illustration. The description is about facial muscle movement or portrayal. Muscles indicate the action done on the facial muscles or the whole head. The emotion expression corresponds to an ascertained combination of some specific action unities, and **Table 3** represents some examples of possible combinations, their description in facial muscles, and the corresponding emotion expression.

In **Table 3**, the combinations of Action Unities are referred to the work of the visual book of group iMOTIONS. For more details, we refer to the above-mentioned review [36] and the work in Refs. [39–42] and references therein.

3.2 Appearance-based features

Local appearance descriptors in the literature are mostly the LBPs (Local Binary Pattern) and its derived, the Local Direction Number pattern (LDN) and the Edge-Oriented Histogram. Local appearance-feature-based methods are used because of their close descriptor of the appearance.

3.2.1 Local binary pattern (LBP)

Local Binary Pattern (LBP) [43] method is a texture operator mostly used in computer vision and image processing applications, such as in object detection, object

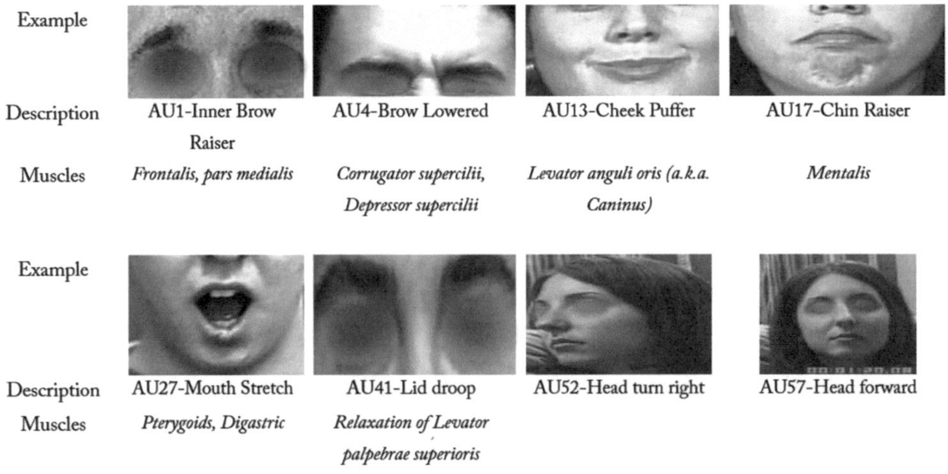

Figure 3.
Examples of action Unity description and muscles involved.

Action Unities combination	Description	Emotion
4 + 5 + 7 + 23	Brow Lowerer, Upper Lid Raiser, Lid Tightener, Lip Tightener	Anger
9 + 15 + 16	Nose Wrinkler, Lip Corner Depressor, Lower Lip Depressor	Disgust
1 + 2 + 4 + 5 + 7 + 20 + 26	Inner Brow Raiser, Outer Brow Raiser, Brow Lowerer, Upper Lid Raiser, Lid Tightener, Lip Stretcher, Jaw Drop	Fear
6 + 12	Cheek Raiser, Lip Corner Puller	Happiness/Joy
1 + 4 + 15	Inner Brow Raiser, Brow Lowerer, Lip Corner Depressor	Sadness
1 + 2 + 5 + 26	Inner Brow Raiser, Outer Brow Raiser, Upper Lid Raiser, Jaw Drop	Surprise

Table 3.
Example of action unities combination for emotion analysis.

tracking, face recognition, and fingerprint matching [44–46]. It is a good operator for real time and very high frame rate applications. The LBP computes features for each image pixel; therefore, real-time extraction of LBP features requires considerable computational performance. It was proposed for a texture analysis [29], and it is insensitive to illumination changes and has an extension to rotation invariant [31].

An LBP feature is a binary vector obtained from a neighborhood around the current image pixel. The basic LBP operator is the 3*3 neighborhood pixels, which is called LBP 8, 1, that is, there are nine pixels with one center and eight neighborhood pixels. The value of the LBP feature is the result of the thresholding of every pixel's luminance against the center pixel's luminance. It is equal to 1 if the difference is positive and to 0 otherwise. The resultant binary number is computed by concatenating all the above binary codes in a clockwise direction, beginning from the top-left one, as shown in **Figure 4**, and the corresponding decimal value is used for labeling [45]. The obtained numbers are known as Local Binary Patterns or LBP codes.

The basic operator of 3*3 neighborhoods is small to capture dominant features with large-scale structures. Later on, Ojala et al. [47] proposed an advanced operator, which is proficient to deal with texture at different scales by using neighborhoods of different sizes. A set of sampling points is evenly spaced on a circle centered at the current pixel to label and define a local neighborhood. A bilinear interpolation permits interpolation of the points that do not fall within the pixels, thus allowing to use a radius of any size and to have any number of sampling points in the neighborhood. Some examples are illustrated in **Figure 5**.

Figure 5 represents an example of LBP extended operator with the circular (8, 1), (16, 2), and (24, 3) neighborhoods.

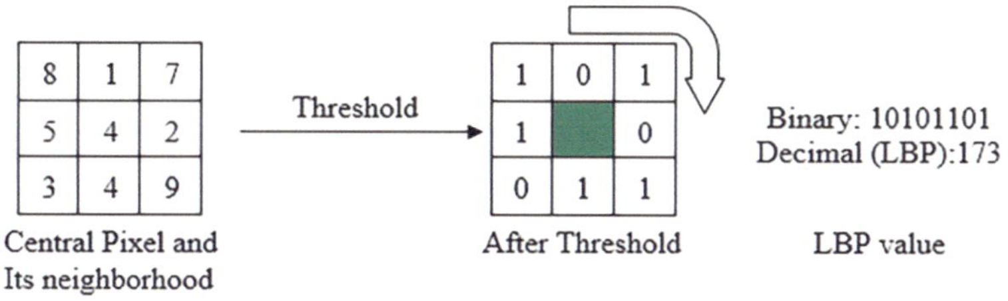

Figure 4.
LBP operator.

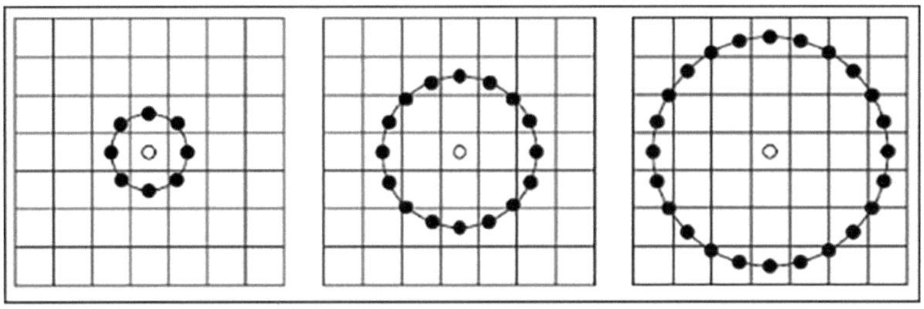

Figure 5.
Examples of the extended LBP operator.

Given a pixel at (x_c, y_c), for an extended LBP $_{(P,\ R)}$ operator with P sampling points neighborhood on a circle of radius R, the LBP can be computed as follows in decimal form:

$$LBP_{(P,R)}(x_c, y_c) = \sum_{P=0}^{P-1} s(i_P - i_c)2^P \tag{1}$$

where i_c and i_p are gray-level values of the central pixel and its neighborhood, the P is the number of surrounding pixels in the circle neighborhood with a radius R, and the function is defined as follows:

$$s(x) = \begin{cases} 1 & if \quad x \geq 0 \\ 0 & if \quad x < 0 \end{cases} \tag{2}$$

The LBP $_{(P,\ R)}$ operator produces 2^P different output values, corresponding to 2^P different binary patterns formed by P pixels in the neighborhood. That makes the extended LBP sensitive to image rotation, and in order to deal with it, a rotation invariant LBP was proposed and is computed as follows:

$$LBP^{ri}_{P,R} = \min\{ROR(LBP_{P,R}, i)|i = 0, 1, \ldots, P-1\} \tag{3}$$

where $ROR(u, i)$ executes a circular by bit right shift on the P-bit number u*i times. This operator computes occurrence statistics of individual rotation invariant patterns corresponding to certain micro-features in the image. It is a good operator for real time and very high frame rate applications.

LBP is invariant against monotonic gray-scale variations and has extensions to rotation invariant texture analysis. In the work of Ojala et al. [47], it was shown that there are patterns containing more information than others do and they were called "uniform patterns" denoted $LBP^{U2}_{(P,R)}$. In fact, it is possible to use a subset of 2^P binary pattern to represent the image's texture. Uniform local binary patterns are the patterns containing at most two bitwise transitions from 0 to 1 or *vice versa* when the corresponding bit string is considered circular. For example,

•00000000 (0 transitions).
•01110000 (2 transitions).
•11,001,111 (2 transitions).
•11,001,001 (4 transitions).
•01010011 (6 transitions).

In natural images, LBP is uniform. The uniform value can be found using the equation below:

$$LBP_{P,R}^{u2} = \begin{cases} \sum_{p=0}^{P-1} s(i_p - i_0), & U(LBP_{P,R}) \leq 2 \\ P(P-1)+2 & otherwise \end{cases} \tag{4}$$

where

$$U(LBP_{P,r}) = |s(i_{P-1} - i_c) - s(i_0 - i_c)| + \sum_{p=1}^{P} |s(i_P - i_c) - s(i_{p-1} - i_c)| \tag{5}$$

If U ≤ 2, it is a uniform LBP otherwise it is nonuniform LBP. The LBP space dimension is reduced from 2^P to P*(P-1) +2 output values. **Figure 6** represents an example of uniform and nonuniform patterns.

However, there have been different improvements in the LBP operator performance, such as improvement of its discriminative capability [48–53], enhancement of its robustness [54, 55], selection of its neighborhood [56–58], extension to 3D data [59–61], and combination with other approaches [62–65]. For more details, we refer to the survey done by Huang et al. [29].

3.2.2 Local directional numbers pattern (LDN)

A Local Directional Numbers Pattern (LDN) is proposed in the work of Rivera et al. [66]. It is a face descriptor that enables to acquire structural information and the intensity variations of the face texture. LDN descriptor extracts features by analysis of all eight (08) directions at every pixel position with a compass mask and generates a code from the analysis of its directional information. From all directions, the top positive and top negative directions are chosen to return a significant descriptor for different textures with similar structural patterns.

Local Directional Number Pattern (LDN) is a six-bit binary code. The resulting feature describes the local primitives, including different types of curves, corners, and junctions, more stably and more informative. They allow making differences in intensity changes in the texture. **Figure 7** represents an example of LDN code computation, and it is proposed in the work of Rivera et al. [66].

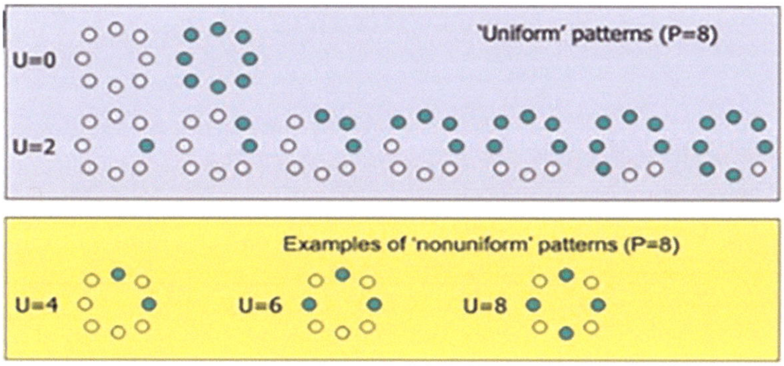

Figure 6.
Uniform and nonuniform patterns.

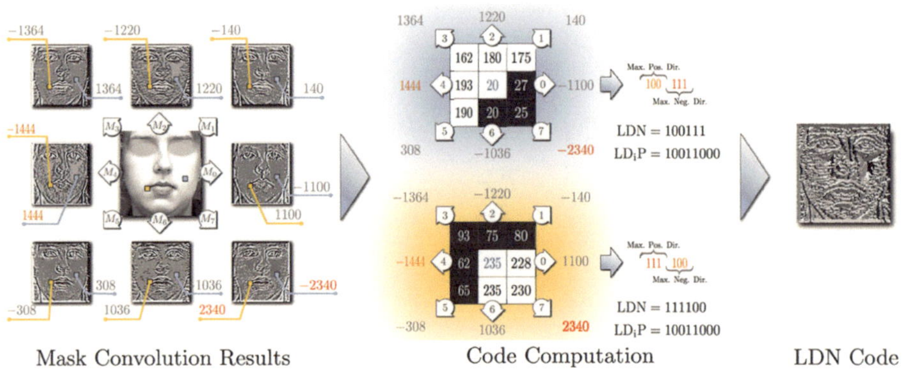

Figure 7.
LDN coding.

The produced code represents information on the texture structure and intensity transitions of each pixel of the input images. The LDN descriptor permits to use of the information of the entire neighborhood, instead of using sparse points. In the coding scheme, LDN code is generated by analyzing the edge response of each mask, representing edge significance in its respective direction, and combining the dominant directional numbers.

Edge responses are not equally important; a high negative or high positive value signals a prominent dark or bright area. The encoding of these outstanding areas is based on the sign information, the top positive directional number represents the three most significant bits in the code and the top negative the three least significant bits. The masks are shown in **Figure 8**; they take names of basic and secondary directions. The code is defined as:

$$LDN_{(x,y)} = 8i_{x,y} + j_{x,y} \tag{6}$$

where (x, y) is the central pixel of the neighborhood to encode, and ix,y and jx,y are directional number maximum positive and minimum negative responses, respectively, which are defined by:

$$\begin{aligned} i_{x,y} &= \arg\max_{i} \left\{ \Pi^{i}(x,y) \mid 0 \leq i \leq 7 \right\} \\ j_{x,y} &= \arg\min_{j} \left\{ \Pi^{j}(x,y) \mid 0 \leq j \leq 7 \right\} \end{aligned} \tag{7}$$

$$\underset{M_0}{\begin{bmatrix} -3 & -3 & 5 \\ -3 & 0 & 5 \\ -3 & -3 & 5 \end{bmatrix}} \underset{M_1}{\begin{bmatrix} -3 & 5 & 5 \\ -3 & 0 & 5 \\ -3 & -3 & -3 \end{bmatrix}} \underset{M_2}{\begin{bmatrix} 5 & 5 & 5 \\ -3 & 0 & -3 \\ -3 & -3 & -3 \end{bmatrix}} \underset{M_3}{\begin{bmatrix} 5 & 5 & -3 \\ 5 & 0 & -3 \\ -3 & -3 & -3 \end{bmatrix}}$$

$$\underset{M_4}{\begin{bmatrix} 5 & -3 & -3 \\ 5 & 0 & -3 \\ 5 & -3 & -3 \end{bmatrix}} \underset{M_5}{\begin{bmatrix} -3 & -3 & -3 \\ 5 & 0 & -3 \\ 5 & 5 & -3 \end{bmatrix}} \underset{M_6}{\begin{bmatrix} -3 & -3 & -3 \\ -3 & 0 & -3 \\ 5 & 5 & 5 \end{bmatrix}} \underset{M_7}{\begin{bmatrix} -3 & -3 & -3 \\ -3 & 0 & 5 \\ -3 & 5 & 5 \end{bmatrix}}$$

Figure 8.
Kirsch edge response masks.

where Π^i is the convolution of the original image, I, and the ith mask, defined by $\Pi^i = I*M^i$.

This approach allows us to distinguish intensity changes (e.g., from bright to dark and *vice versa*) in the texture that otherwise will be missed most evident directions descriptor uses the information of the whole neighborhood, it does not use sparse points for its computation as it is for LBP. LDN translates the directional information of the face's textures (i.e., the texture's structure) in a compact way, producing a more discriminative code.

3.2.3 Edge orientation histogram

Edge Orientation Histogram (EOH) engenders a feature set extracted based on the gradient of the pixels that correspond to edges of an image. It is used as a descriptor in classification or detection tasks. These descriptors rely on the abundance of the information of edge and are invariant to global illumination [67–69]. The edge is computed by filtering the gray-scale image using the Sobel operator. Five operators provide information about the strength of the gradient in five particular directions, as represented in **Figure 9**.

Figure 9 represents the Sobel mask for five directions; in (a) it is the vertical direction, (b) it is the horizontal direction, (c) and (d) are the diagonals directions, and (e) it is the non-direction case. The gradient pixels are classified into β images corresponding to β orientation ranges; they are also designated as bins. Therefore, a pixel in bin $k_n \in \beta$ contains its gradient magnitude if its orientation is inside β's range, otherwise it is null. Integral images are now used to store the accumulation image of each of the edge bins. **Figure 10** represents the Edge Orientation Histogram.

−1	−2	−1	−1	0	+1	2	2	−1	−1	2	2	−1	0	1
0	0	0	−2	0	+2	2	−1	−1	−1	−1	2	0	0	0
+1	+2	+1	−1	0	+1	−1	−1	−1	−1	−1	−1	1	0	−1
	(a)			(b)			(c)			(d)			(e)	

Figure 9.
Sobel mask for five directions [70].

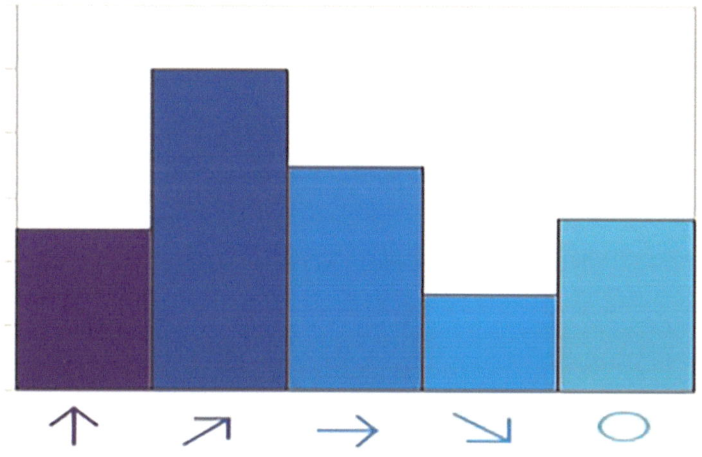

Figure 10.
Edge orientation histogram [70].

Though these two feature extraction approaches are mostly present in the literature but there are other works that considered hybrid approach [71]. A hybrid method means to at the same time use of appearance features and other shape features to make them complementary. Mixing these two types of features will improve classifier performance.

3.3 Feature extraction method classification

The facial expression recognition rate is more influenced by the basic features used for classifier training. From different works on facial feature extraction research, there are two main categories of feature extraction methods as mentioned above: geometric based and appearance based. In this work, we propose **Table 4** for a classification.

From this classification in **Table 4**, there are mainly two categories of feature extraction: appearance based and geometric based. Different cited methods

Feature category	Feature details	Techniques	References	Applications
Geometric based	FFP	Active Appearance Model (AAM)	Ratliff & Patterson [38]	Texture and Shape
		Active Shape Model (ASM)	Iqtait et al. [72]	Shape
	FACS	Holistic spatial analysis based on PCA, Feature-based approach and Facial motion analysis	Tian et al. [39]	Action Units
		Convolutional Experts Constrained Local Model (CE-CLM) and Histograms of Oriented Gradients (HOG	Yang et al. [40]	Geometric and appearance features
Appearance based	LBP	Improved LBP (Mean LBP)	Jin et al. [48], Bai et al. [49]	Effects of central pixels
		Hamming LBP	Yang and Wang [50]	Decrease of error rate caused by noise disturbances
		Extended LBP	Huang et al. [51]	Deals with variations of illumination
		Completed LBP	Guo et al. [53]	Better texture classification for rotation invariant
		Local Ternary Patterns	Tan and Triggs [54]	Discriminant and less sensitive to noise in uniform regions
		Soft LBP	Ahonen and Pietikäinen [55]	Robust to noise and output continuous according to input
		Elongated LBP	Liao and Chung [56]	New feature Average Maximum Distance Gradient Magnitude (AMDGM)

Feature category	Feature details	Techniques	References	Applications
		FMulti-Block LBP	Liao and Si [57]	More robust and consider integral image
		Three/Four Patch LBP	Wolf et al. [58]	Improves multi-option identification and same/not-same classification
		3D LBP	Fehr [59]	Texture analysis in 3D
		Volume LBP	Zhao and Pietikäinen [61]	Combines motion and appearance
		LBP and SIFT	Heikkilä et al. [63]	Tolerance to lighting changes, robustness on even image areas, and computational efficiency
		LBP and Gabor wavelet	Zhang et al. [73]	No need training procedure to build the face model
			He et al. [62]	
		LBP Histogram Fourier	Ahonen et al. [65]	Rotation invariant image descriptor
	EOH	Haar wavelet and EOH	Gerónimo et al. [67]	Object change in cluttered environments
		EOH for smile	Timotius and Setyawan [69]	Discriminate lip to depict a smile
	LDN	LDN basic	Rivera et al. [66]	Directional information of the face textures
		LDPv	Kabir et al. [10]	texture and contrast information of facial components

Table 4.
Classification of different feature extraction methods.

or techniques are used for facial expression feature extraction as well as other feature extraction-related work [68]. Among geometric feature extraction, the active appearance model is mostly used combined with the principal component analysis method to reduce the vector dimension for efficient application in real time. Among the appearance-based feature extraction, the local-based pattern algorithm is the mostly found in the literature and highly expended.

In recent work, in view of collecting enough features to enhance facial expression recognition rate by including more details, researchers propose hybrid methods [71, 72].

4. Conclusions

Automatic facial emotion recognition is a recent research trend that is applied in many areas, such as security, health, education, and social interaction. Facial feature extraction is one of the crucial steps in order to get a good and quick classifier at the end. In view of getting a performant classifier firstly, facial feature representation has to distinguish different individuals well and at the same time tolerate that there can be minor variation within-class members. It should be easy to be extracted from the basic facial images to speed up further processing; all that demands is that the final sample space must stay in a low dimensional space to reduce classification complexity.

This work pictures different methods used in facial feature extraction and their best usage. It can serve as a reference and guide to researchers in facial expression recognition. Hereby, cited methods are mainly applied to 2D images and but works considering 3D mage are also related. Actually, as devices are getting smarter and averaging natural perception, it is a judiciary that the corresponding software development follows.

Author details

Michele Mukeshimana*, Abraham Niyongere and Jérémie Ndikumagenge
Research Center in Infrastructure, Environment and Technology (CRIET), University of Burundi, Bujumbura city, Republic of Burundi

*Address all correspondence to: michele.mukeshimana@ub.edu.bi

References

[1] Cheng X, Zhan Q, Wang J, Ma R. A high recognition rate of feature extraction algorithm without segmentation. In: Proceeding of IEEE 6th International Conference on Industrial Engineering and Applications (ICIEA). Tokyo, Japan: IEEE; 12-15 April, 2019. pp. 923-927. DOI: 10.1109/IEA.2019.8714943

[2] Picard RW. Affective Computing. United States of America (USA): MIT Press, MIT Media Laboratory Perceptual Computing Section Technical Report No 321; 1997

[3] Picard RW. Affective computing: From laughter to IEEE. IEEE Transactions on Affective Computing. Jan. 2010, vol. 1, no. 1, pp. 11-17. DOI: 10.1109/T-AFFC.2010.10

[4] Kamarol SKA, Jaward MH, Parkkinen J, Parthiban R. Spatiotemporal feature extraction for facial expression recognition. IET Image Processing. 2016; **10**(7):534-541

[5] Li SZ, Jain AK, editors. Handbook of Face Recognition. London Limited: Springer-Verlag; 2011. DOI: 10.1007/978-0-85729-932-1_4

[6] Han J, Kamber M, Pei J. Data preprocessing. In: Data Mining: Concepts and Techniques. Waltham, MA, USA: Elsevier Inc.; 2012. pp. 84-124

[7] Theodoridis S, Koutroumbas K. Feature selection. Pattern Recognition. 4th ed. Boston: Academic Press; 2009

[8] Shan C, Gong S, McOwan P. Robust facial expression recognition using local binary patterns. In: Proceedings of IEEE International Conference Image Processing. Genova Italy: IEEE; 14-14 September 2005. pp. 914-917

[9] Keche J-K, Dhore MP. Facial feature expression based approach for human face recognition: A review. International Journal of Innovative Science Engineering & Technology. 2014;**1**(3):1-5

[10] Kabir H, Jabid T, Chae O. Local directional pattern variance (LDPv): A robust feature descriptor for facial expression recognition. The International Arab Journal of Information Technology. 2012;**9**(4): 1-10

[11] Vertegaal R, Slagter R, van der Veer G, et al. Eye gaze patterns in conversations: There is more to conversational agents than meets the eyes. In: Proceedings of the SIGCHI Conference on Human Factors in Computing Systems. Seattle, WA, USA: ACM Press; 2001. pp. 301-308

[12] Karpouzis, K. Editorial: "Signals to Signs" – Feature Extraction, Recognition, and Multimodal Fusion. In: Cowie R, Pelachaud C, Petta P, editors. Emotion-Oriented Systems. Cognitive Technologies. Berlin, Heidelberg: Springer; 2011. pp. 65-70 DOI: 10.1007/978-3-642-15184-2_5

[13] Guyon I, Elisseeff A. An introduction to feature extraction. Guyon I et al, editor. Feature Extraction, Studies in Fuzziness and Soft Computing. vol. 207. New York: Springer; 2006. pp. 1-25

[14] Cruz A, Garcia D, Pires G, et al. Facial Expression Recognition Based on EOG toward Emotion Detection for Human-Robot Interaction. In:

Proceedings of BIOSIGNALS. Lisbon, Portugal: SciTePress; 2015. pp. 31-37

[15] Sadr J, Jarudi I, Sinha P. The role of eyebrows in face recognition. Perception. 2003;**32**:285-293

[16] Rani PI, Muneeswaran K. Facial emotion recognition based on eye and mouth regions. International Journal Pattern Recognition and Artificial Intelligence. 2015;**30**(2016):1655020. DOI: 10.1142/S021800141655020X

[17] Li ZJ, Duan XD, Wang CR. Automatic expression recognition based on mouth shape analysis. Applied Mechanics and Materials. 2014;**644-650**: 4018-4022

[18] Hasan HS, Kareem SBA. Gesture feature extraction for static gesture recognition. Arabian Journal for Science and Engineering. 2013;**38**:3349. DOI: 10.1007/s13369-013-0654-6

[19] Graves A, Schmidhuber J, Mayer C, et al. Facial expression recognition with recurrent neural networks. In: International Workshop on Cognition for Technical Systems. Munich, Germany: coTeSys; 2008

[20] Vukadinovic D, Pantic M. Fully automatic facial feature point detection using Gabor feature based boosted classifiers. In: Proceedings of the IEEE International Conference on Systems, Man and Cybernetics Waikoloa, Hawaii. October 10-12, 2005

[21] Bhatta LK, Rana D. Facial feature extraction of color image using gray scale intensity value. International Journal of Engineering Research & Technology (IJERT). 2014;**3**(3):1177-1180

[22] Huang ZQ, Chen L, Harper M. An open source prosodic feature extraction tool. In: Proceedings of the Language Resources and Evaluation Conference (LREC'2006). Genoa, Italy: European Language Resources Association (ELRA); 2006. pp. 2116-2121

[23] Pantic M, Caridakis G, André E, et al. Multimodal emotion recognition from low-level cues. In: P. Petta Pelachaud C, Cowie R, editors. Emotion-Oriented Systems, Cognitive Technologies, C©. Berlin, Heidelberg: Springer-Verlag; 2011. DOI 10.1007/978-3-642-15184-2_8

[24] Cowie R, Douglas-Cowie E, Savvidou S, et al. FEELTRACE: An instrument for recording perceived emotion in real time. In: Proceedings of the ISCA Workshop on Speech and Emotion: A Conceptual Framework for Research. Belfast, Ireland: ISCA; 2000. pp. 19-24

[25] Eyben F, Wöllmer M, Schuller B. Open EAR-introducing the Munich open-source emotion and affect recognition toolkit. In: Proceedings of the Third International Conference on Affective Computing and Intelligent Interaction and Workshops (ACII 2009). Amsterdam, Netherlands: De Rode Hoed; 2009. pp. 1-6

[26] Eyben F, Wöllmer M, Schuller B. openSMILE-the Munich versatile and fast open-source audio feature extractor. In: Proceedings of the 18th ACM International Conference on Multimedia (MM'10). Firenze, Italy: Association for Computing Machinery (ACM); 2010. pp. 1459-1462

[27] Grimm M, Kroschel K, Narayanan S. The Vera am Mittag German audio-visual emotional speech database. In: Proceeding of the IEEE International Conference on Multimedia and Expo (ICME). Hannover, Germany: Institute of Electrical and Electronics Engineers (IEEE); 2008. pp. 865-868

[28] Castellano G, Kessous L, Caridakis G. Emotion recognition through multiple modalities: Face, body gesture, and speech. In: Christian P, Beale R, editors. Affect and Emotion in HCI. Vol. 4868. Springer: Berlin, of the series LNCS; 2008. pp. 92-103

[29] Huang D, Shan C-F, Ardebilian M, et al. Local binary patterns and its application to facial image analysis: A survey. IEEE Transactions on Systems, Man, and Cybernetics, Part C (Applications and Reviews). 2011;**41**(6):765-781

[30] Kipp M. Anvil - a generic annotation tool for multimodal dialogue. In: Proceedings of Eurospeech. Aalborg, Denmark: Citeseer; 2001. pp. 1367-1370

[31] Mohamed E, ElGamal A, Ghoneim R, et al. Local binary patterns as texture descriptors for user attitude recognition. International Journal of Computer Science and Network Security (IJCSNS). 2010;**10**(6):222-229

[32] Wu YM, Wang HW, Lu YL, Yen S, Hsiao YT, Pan JS, et al. Intelligent Information and Database Systems. ACIIDS 2012. Lecture Notes in Computer Science, vol. 7196. Berlin, Heidelberg: Springer. pp. 228-238. DOI: 10.1007/978-3-642-28487-8_23

[33] Tian YL, Kanade T, Cohn JF. Facial Expression Analysis: Handbook of Face Recognition. New York, NY: Springer; 2005. DOI: 10.1007/0-387-27257-7_12

[34] Sumathi CP, Santhanam T, Mahadevi M. Automatic facial expression analysis a survey. International Journal of Computer Science & Engineering Survey (IJCSES). 2012;**3**(6):259-275

[35] Cootes TF, Edwards GJ, Taylor CJ. Active appearance models. In: Proceedings of the Fifth European Conference on Computer Vision (ECCV'98). Vol. 1407. Freiburg, Germany: LNCS; 1998. pp. 484-498

[36] Wu C-H, Lin J-C, Wei W-L. Survey on audiovisual emotion recognition: Databases, features, and data fusion strategies. APSIPA Transactions on Signal and Information Processing. 2014; **2014**(3):e12

[37] Ahdid R, Taifi K, Safi S, Manaut B. A survey on facial feature points detection techniques and approaches. International Journal of Computer and Information Engineering. 2016;**10**(8):1-8

[38] Ratliff MS, Patterson E. Emotion recognition using facial expressions with active appearance models. In: Proceedings of HCI 2008 (HCI). Liverpool, UK: Citeseer; 1-5 September 2008. pp. 89-98

[39] Tian Y-L, Kanade T, Cohn J-F. Recognizing AUs for facial expression analysis. IEEE Transactions on Pattern Analysis and Machine Intelligence. 2001; **23**(2):91-116

[40] Yang J, Zhang F, Chen B, Khan SU. Facial Expression Recognition Based on Facial Action Unit. In :Proceedings of the Tenth International Green and Sustainable Computing Conference (IGSC). Alexandria, VA, USA: IEEE, October 21-24, 2019. pp. 1-6. DOI: 10.1109/IGSC48788.2019.8957163.2019:1-6

[41] Hager JC. A comparison of units for visually measuring facial actions. Behavior Research Methods Instruments & Computers. 1985;**17**(4):450-468

[42] Friesen E, Ekman P. Measuring facial movement. Journal of Nonverbal Behavior 1. 1976;**1976**:56–75

[43] Ojala T, Pietikäinen M, Harwood D. A comparative study of texture measures with classification based on featured

distributions [J]. Pattern Recognition. 1996;**29**(1):51-59

[44] Mukeshimana M, Ban X-J, Karani N. Toward instantaneous facial expression recognition using privileged information. International Journal of Computer Techniques. 2016;**3**(6):23-29

[45] López MB, Nieto A, Boutellier J, et al. Evaluation of real-time LBP computing in multiple architectures. Journal of Real-Time Image Processing. 2017;**13**(2):375-396

[46] Pietikäinen M, Hadid A, Zhao G, et al. Lbp in different applications. Computer Vision Using Local Binary Patterns. 2011;**40**:193-204

[47] Ojala T, Pietikäinen M, Maenpaa T. Multiresolution gray-scale and rotation invariant texture classification with local binary patterns. IEEE Trans Pattern Analysis and Machine Intelligence. 2002; **24**(7):971-987

[48] Jin H, Liu Q, Lu H, et al. Face detection using improved LBP under Bayesian framework. In: Proceeding of International Conference on Image and Graphics (ICIG). Hong Kong, China: Institute of Electrical and Electronics Engineers (IEEE); 2004. pp. 306-309

[49] Bai G, Zhu Y, Ding Z. A hierarchical face recognition method based on local binary pattern. In: Proc. Congress on Image and Signal Processing. Sanya, Hainan, China: Institute of Electrical and Electronics Engineers (IEEE); 2008. pp. 610-614

[50] Yang H, Wang Y. A LBP-based Face Recognition Method with Hamming Distance Constraint. In: Proceedings of the International Conference on Image and Graphics (ICIG 2007), Chengdu, China. 2007. pp. 645-649. DOI: 10.1109/ICIG.2007.144

[51] Huang D, Wang Y, Wang Y. A robust method for near infrared face recognition based on extended local binary pattern. In: Proc. Int. Symposium on Visual Computing (ISVC). Las Vegas, Nevada, USA: Springer Berlin Heidelberg; 2007. pp. 437-446

[52] Huang Y, Wang Y, Tan T. Combining statistics of geometrical and correlative features for 3D face recognition. In: Proc. British Machine Vision Conference (BMVC). Edinburgh, UK: Citeseer; 2006. pp. 879-888

[53] Guo Z, Zhang L, Zhang D. A completed modeling of local binary pattern operator for texture classification. IEEE Transactions on Image Processing (TIP). 2010;**19**(6): 1657-1663

[54] Tan X, Triggs B. Enhanced local texture feature sets for face recognition under difficult lighting conditions. In: Proc. Analysis and Modeling of Faces and Gestures (AMFG). Rio de Janeiro, Brazil: Springer Berlin Heidelberg; 2007. pp. 168-182

[55] Ahonen T, Pietikäinen M. Soft histograms for local binary patterns. In: Proc. Finnish Signal Processing Symposium (FINSIG). Finland: Citeseer; 2007. pp. 1-4

[56] Liao S, Chung ACS. Face recognition by using elongated local binary patterns with average maximum distance gradient magnitude. In: Proc. Asian Conf. Computer Vision (ACCV). Tokyo, Japan: Springer Berlin Heidelberg; 2007. pp. 672-679

[57] Liao S, Li SZ. Learning multi-scale block local binary patterns for face recognition. In: Proceedings of the International Conference on Biometrics. Seoul, Korea: Springer Berlin Heidelberg; 2007. pp. 828-837

[58] Wolf L, Hassner T, Taigman Y. Descriptor based methods in the wild. In: Proc. ECCV Workshop on Faces in 'Real-Life' Images: Detection, Alignment, and Recognition. Marseille, France: INRIA; 2008

[59] Fehr J. Rotational invariant uniform local binary patterns for full 3D volume texture analysis. In: Proc. Finnish Signal Processing Symposium (FINSIG). Finland: Citeseer; 2007

[60] Paulhac L, Makris P, Ramel J-Y. Comparison between 2D and 3D local binary pattern methods for characterization of three-dimensional textures. In: Proc. Int. Conf. Image Analysis and Recognition. Póvoa de Varzim, Portugal: Springer Berlin Heidelberg; 2008

[61] Zhao G, Pietikäinen M. Dynamic texture recognition using local binary patterns with an application to facial expressions. IEEE Transactions on Pattern Analysis and Machine Intelligence. 2007;**29**(6):915-928

[62] He L, Zou C, Zhao L, et al. An enhanced LBP feature based on facial expression recognition. In: IEEE Engineering in Medicine and Biology Society 27th Annual Conference. IEEE; 2005. pp. 3300-3303

[63] Heikkilä M, Pietikäinen M, Schmid C. Description of interest regions with local binary patterns. Pattern Recognition. 2009;**42**(3):425-436

[64] Huang D, Zhang G, Ardabilian M, et al. 3D face recognition using distinctiveness enhanced facial representations and local feature hybrid matching. In: Proc. IEEE International Conference on Bio-Metrics: Theory, Applications and Systems. Washington DC, USA: Institute of Electrical and Electronics Engineers (IEEE); 2010. pp. 1-7

[65] Ahonen T, Matas J, He C, et al. Rotation invariant image description with local binary pattern histogram fourier features. In: Proc. Scandinavian Conference on Image Analysis (SCIA). Oslo, Norway: Springer Berlin Heidelberg; 2009. pp. 61-70

[66] Rivera AR, Castillo RJ, Chae OO. Local directional number pattern for face analysis: Face and expression recognition. IEEE Transactions on Image Processing. 2013;**22**(5):1740-1752. DOI: 10.1109/TIP.2012.2235848

[67] Gerónimo D, López A, Ponsa D, et al. Haar wavelets and edge orientation histograms for on-board pedestrian detection. Martí J, et al, editors. IbPRIA. Berlin, Heidelberg: Springer-Verlag; 2007. pp. 418-425

[68] Alefs B, Eschemann G, Ramoser H, Beleznai C. Road Sign Detection from Edge Orientation Histograms. IEEE Intelligent Vehicles Symposium. 2007. pp. 993-998. DOI: 10.1109/IVS.2007.4290246

[69] Timotius IK, Setyawan I. Evaluation of edge orientation histograms in smile detection. In: Proceedings of the 6th International Conference on Information Technology and Electrical Engineering (ICITEE). Yogyakarta, Indonesia: IEEE; 2014. pp. 1-5. DOI: 10.1109/ICITEED.2014.7007905

[70] Edge orientation histograms in global and local features (Octave_Matlab) - that doesn't make any sense [Internet]. Available from: http://robertour.com/2012/01/26/edge-orientation-histograms-in-global-and-local-features/ revisited on December 9th, 2022

[71] Kaul A, Chauhan S, Arora AS. Hybrid approach for facial feature extraction. International Journal of

Engineering Research & Technology (IJERT). 2016;**4**(15):1-3

[72] Iqtait M, Mohamad FS, Mamat M. Feature extraction for face recognition via active shape model (ASM) and active appearance model (AAM). In proceedings of IOP Conf. Series: Materials Science and Engineering. 2018; **332**:012032. DOI: 10.1088/1757-899X/332/1/012032

[73] Zhang W, Shan S, Gao W, Chen X, Zhang H. Local Gabor binary pattern histogram sequence (LGBPHS): A novel non-statistical model for face representation and recognition. In: Proceedings of the IEEE International Conference of Computer Vision (ICCV). Beijing. PR China: Institute of Electrical and Electronics Engineers (IEEE); 17-21 October 2005. pp. 786-791

Chapter 5

Emotional Intelligence of Korean Students and Its Recent Research Trends

Soo-Koung Jun and Sook Hee Ryue

Abstract

In Korea, emotional intelligence is based on the concept and components proposed by John Mayer and Peter Salovey, and the model proposed by Professor Moon Yong-Rin is the most widely used. Moon Young-Rin defined the concept of emotional intelligence as the ability of mental process to evaluate and express one's own emotions of others, to regulate emotions, and to use emotions in a socially adaptive way. 4 domain 16 factor model is the most widely used in Korea: Recognition and expression of emotions; Emotional thinking promotion; Use of emotional knowledge; and Reflective regulation of emotions. Emotional intelligence is reported to be deeply related to creative disposition and positively correlated with academic achievement. For healthy student education, the measurement, education, and training of emotional intelligence should be studied and improved continually in Korean society. Future researches to find out Koreans' unique emotions and structure are hoped to continued.

Keywords: emotional intelligence, South Korea, Korean students, emotional quotient, creativity

1. Introduction

What are the essential requirements that an individual must have to grow into a healthy member of society and realize a successful career as a protagonist of a more meaningful life? Amid technological development and the flood of information, the educational foundation for talent development is overflowing with various opportunities. Nevertheless, the road to raising a healthy and happy member of society seems increasingly far and arduous.

Twenty-three years after entering the new world of the twenty-first century, we constantly look back to see if the academic almighty, which still believes that happiness is in the order of grades, is producing lonely and selfish half-talented people in the ever-changing educational system. Amid uncertain future social changes, children who should be happy are exhausted from early education and excessive prior learning. Thanks to anxious parents and marketing of private education, children's bodies, and minds, which should be healthy, are slowly getting sick while struggling to become smart and smart. The downward trend in the age of exposure to increasing youth crime and delinquency is just one unfortunate aspect.

In modern society, where crimes caused by various mental pathologies are increasing day by day, the limitations of traditional academic supremacy education have been felt, and accordingly, the school has come to recognize the importance and necessity of character education for students. Research on emotional intelligence is being emphasized as a key component of character education [1]. In other words, as society becomes more complex and accelerated, failure to develop the ability to cope with the changes of the times can lead to depression and emotional instability of maladjustment [2]. Emotional intelligence is required to succeed and cope adaptively in the rapidly changing modern society and organizational society [3]. Therefore, it is expected that discussions on emotional intelligence will continue in the future for a happy and healthy life.

Emotional intelligence is an integrated ability to solve various problems by thinking and using emotions cognitively. It is one of the intellectual abilities that must be developed in order to realize a successful career for a healthy and happy life in the modern society's unlimited competition system. The ability to understand one's own and others' emotions and to control one's own emotions is required in order to establish desirable interpersonal relationships as a healthy member of society and to control one's own emotions. When infancy and childhood are said to be a critical period for emotional intelligence development [4], it is very important to measure, educate, and develop emotional intelligence during this period.

On the other hand, the university student period is a preparation process for social advancement, and it is a period to learn various human relationships and acquire knowledge and skills in the major field [5]. In other words, college students must perform tasks for their future, unlike previous passive and standardized middle and high schools, and society tends to expect college students to change their roles as adults [6]. However, for university students who are not sufficiently prepared as adults, this autonomy and responsibility can cause various stresses. In other words, college students, who are in a period of independence from their parents, choosing a job and preparing for transition to the world of work, may have psychological problems such as anxiety and frustration [7].

As the end of education, entry into the work world, and economic and social independence, which are the criteria for distinguishing adolescents from young people in modern society, are being transferred to those in their late 20s or 30s, many college students still experience confusion, conflict, and stress. It has been shown to have the characteristics of experiencing adolescents [8]. In addition, many researchers reported that these conflicts and stress experienced by college students are harmful to mental health [8]. In other words, college students experience a delayed process of social maturation compared to biological maturation, and in particular, this is a prominent feature of college students in Korea [6].

2. Literature review

2.1 Conceptual background on emotional intelligence

Emotional intelligence, as opposed to general intelligence, refers to the ability to control emotions and feelings. Emotional intelligence is not the ability to think, remember, calculate, or reason, but rather the emotional capacity that enables or suppresses and limits such abilities. When angry, the emotional intelligence of a person who explodes and radiates this to harm others and commits harm to himself is significantly lower than those who do not.

Imagine there are some students having homework that needs to be done by tomorrow, but do not want to do it, there are students who hesitate and cannot do it in the end, and there are students who clenched their teeth and persisted. Students who persevere in completing homework they do not want to do like this while appeasing themselves can be said to have higher emotional intelligence than students who do not [9].

The term emotional intelligence was first used in 1990 by Professor John Mayer of the University of New Hampshire and Professor Peter Salovey of Yale University, USA. Introducing EQ (Emotional Quotient), the term EQ (Emotional Quotient) spread through the mass media, and as a result, countless books were published and gained popularity [1]. In addition, the concept of emotional intelligence is used interchangeably with various terms such as emotional literacy, emotional competence, emotional quotient, and personal intelligence [10]. In Korea, EI (Emotional Intelligence) or EQ (Emotional Quotient) is used interchangeably with two name, The term of emotion or affect is a concept that has been commonly used among scholars for a relatively long time, and also, the term "emotion' is the "characteristics" and "trait" of personality rather than the meaning of "ability" and "skill" [11].

Aristotle emphasized the importance of controlling emotions with intellect in Nicomachean Ethics and Thorndike in the 1920s specified a concept related to emotional intelligence under the name of 'social intelligence' [12]. Social intelligence refers to the ability to perceive one's own and others' internal states, motives, and behaviors, and to act appropriately based on that information. There are Epstein's 'constructive thinking' and Cantor's 'social problem solving' that have been proposed as sub-factors of social intelligence. Like these, it can be said that it is the ability to deal with social problems in which emotions and feelings are intervened [12].

Even after that, psychologists have been steadily studying other intelligences other than those that can be measured by IQ, and Gardner's theory of multiple intelligences is a representative example. Emotional intelligence is also a concept similar to 'personal intelligence' in Gardner's theory of multiple intelligences. Gardner's multiple intelligences are linguistic intelligence, logical-mathematical intelligence, musical intelligence, spatial intelligence, body-kinesthetic intelligence, natural intelligence, interpersonal intelligence, and intrapersonal intelligence. Among them, interpersonal intelligence and intrapersonal intelligence are combined and called 'personal intelligence'. 'Interpersonal intelligence' means the ability to discriminate and recognize the moods, temperaments, motives, and desires of others and respond appropriately. And intra-individual intelligence means the ability to examine and discriminate one own's various emotions, and to use the information obtained from this as a means of understanding and guiding one's own behavior.

Afterwards, it was in 1990 that John Mayer, a psychology professor at the University of New Hampshire, and Peter Salovey, a professor at Yale University, began to establish a systematic theory on emotional intelligence by comprehensively considering scattered studies in various fields related to it. According to Salovey and Mayer [13], emotional intelligence is a sub-factor of social intelligence, "the ability to evaluate and express one's own and others' emotions, the ability to effectively regulate one's own and others' emotions, and the ability to use and use those emotions to plan and fulfill one's life."

Emotional intelligence began to attract public attention as the concept of EQ after Daniel Goleman treated his book "Emotional Intelligence" as a cover story in Time magazine (October 9, 1995). It predicts the possibility of human success by relying on cognitive abilities measured by standardized tests such as tests or SAT (Scholastic Aptitude Test), criticizes the tradition that has been used as a basis for education, and introduces the concept of emotional intelligence.

Emotional intelligence is a concept that combines two elements: 'emotion' and 'intelligence'. 'Intelligence' in emotional intelligence implies the meaning of ability, and this point is the same concept as the meaning of intelligence that generally spoken of. However, the difference between the meaning of intelligence in emotional intelligence and the meaning of general intelligence is the mechanism and manifestation of emotional intelligence [13].

'Emotion' in emotional intelligence focuses on the aspect that helps and promotes human thinking and cognitive processes. According to Salovey and Mayer [14], intense emotional response enhances the function of intelligence by interrupting ongoing information processing and allowing us to focus on important information. In other words, it is assumed that emotions activate thinking more intelligently and that these emotions contain knowledge about the relationship between people and the world. Emotion is a complex state that involves perception of a certain object or situation and accompanying physiological or behavioral changes, and is a higher level concept that includes various emotions. Emotion can function as a source of personal information, and it is believed that knowing and expressing one's emotions accurately plays an important role in an individual's adaptive ability [13].

2.2 Components and research of emotional intelligence

The emotional intelligence model can be divided into a competency model that considers emotional intelligence as a single ability and a mixed model that includes personality traits. The competency model views emotional intelligence as intelligence or ability related to emotions, and the mixed model is a comprehensive view that includes personality traits [1, 4, 15]. Each researcher reports the concept of emotional intelligence and various components. The definition of emotional intelligence in major preceding studies is shown in **Table 1**.

Researcher	Perspective	Details
Mayer and Salovey [13]	Competency model	The ability to accurately evaluate and express one's own and others' emotions, the ability to effectively regulate one's own and others' emotions, and the ability to use and utilize emotions to achieve one's own life
Goleman [4]	Mixed model	Ability to recognize one's own and others' emotions, to motivate oneself, and to deal with one's own and others' emotions
Mayer and Salovey [14]	Competency model	The ability to accurately recognize, evaluate, and express emotions, the ability to promote thinking through emotions, the ability to understand emotions and emotional knowledge, and the ability to regulate emotions to promote emotional and intellectual growth
Bar-on [15]	Mixed model	The ability to respond appropriately to the demands and pressures of the environment, including non-cognitive abilities, talents, and skills
Wong and Law [16]	Competency model	The ability to perceive, evaluate, and express one's emotions, the ability to promote thinking through emotions, the ability to understand emotions, and the ability to control emotions for emotional and intellectual growth
Moon [17]	Competency model	The ability of mental processes to evaluate and express one's own emotions of others, to regulate emotions, and to use emotions in a socially adaptive way

Table 1.
Definitions of emotional intelligence.

First, from the perspective of the competency model, Salovey and Mayer [13] conceptualized the term Emotional Intelligence for the first time. Emotional intelligence is defined as the ability to accurately evaluate and express one's own and others' emotions, the ability to effectively regulate one's own and others' emotions, and the ability to use and utilize emotions to plan and achieve one's life. In addition, this definition explains emotions as emotional abilities and sets up three processes that include emotional processes. Thus, the initial concept of emotional intelligence is significant in that it highlighted the aspect of emotional intelligence. However, along with criticism on issues such as discrimination from general intelligence and connectivity between components, it was also argued that the concepts of social intelligence and emotional intelligence are not very different [9, 14]. In addition, there was criticism that the concept of emotional intelligence and the ambiguity of its components were not included, as well as the thinking part for emotion [1, 9].

To compensate for these limitations, Mayer and Salovey [14] presented a clearer and more robust concept of emotional intelligence. In other words, emotional intelligence is the ability to accurately recognize, evaluate, and express emotions, the ability to promote thinking through emotions, the ability to understand emotions and emotional knowledge, and the ability to regulate emotions to promote emotional and intellectual growth. It was defined as the ability to do things [7]. In addition, they proposed an emotional intelligence system consisting of four domains of emotional intelligence and four abilities in each domain.

In a similar context, from the perspective of the competency model, Wong and Law [16] defined emotional intelligence as the ability to accurately perceive, evaluate, and express one's emotions, the ability to promote thinking through emotion, the ability to understand emotional knowledge, and emotional intelligence. · It was defined as the ability to control emotions for intellectual growth. In addition, based on the concept of emotional intelligence defined by Mayer and Salovey [14], emotional intelligence was composed of self-emotional recognition, recognition of others' emotions, emotional regulation, and emotional utilization.

Meanwhile, from the viewpoint of the mixed model, Goleman [4] defined emotional intelligence as a concept that includes talent and personality traits. Accordingly, emotional intelligence was defined as the ability to recognize one's own and others' emotions, motivate oneself, and handle one's own and others' emotions well [4]. In addition, he consisted of self-emotional recognition, emotional recognition of others, motivation, emotional regulation, and interpersonal skills as components of emotional intelligence. Accordingly, emotional intelligence was viewed as five domains that recognize one's own emotions and those of others, motivate oneself, and regulate emotions in relationships with others [4]. Goleman also divided emotional intelligence into personal competence and social competence. Personal competence includes self-awareness and self-emotional regulation, and social competence includes empathy and social skills [18]. This can be seen as extending emotional intelligence to motivation, other talents, or personality traits. In addition, compared to Salovey and Mayer's [13] emotional intelligence, emotional recognition and emotional utilization are similar, but their characteristics are that they have been extended to the ability to motivate oneself for one's own goals.

In a similar perspective, Bar-on [15] defined emotional intelligence as a set of non-cognitive abilities, talents, and skills as the ability to respond appropriately to environmental demands and pressures [15]. In addition, Bar-on integrated factors for social and practical intelligence into emotional intelligence. These concepts include intrapersonal skills, interpersonal skills, adaptability, stress management, and general mood. In addition, problem solving, flexibility, and responsibility necessary for social success are included in each subdomain. Specifically, personal skills include emotional self-awareness, self-assertion, self-realization, and independence; interpersonal skills include relationships with others, responsibility, and empathy; adaptability includes problem-solving skills, reality testing, and flexibility; and stress control includes stress Perseverance, control, and general mood consist of happiness and optimism. Therefore, even in the case of Bar-On [15], it can be seen as a mixed model that integrates various psychological factors, including intellectual ability and personality characteristics.

However, the concept definition of the mixed model, including Goleman, made the concept of emotional intelligence rather ambiguous as it failed to provide a basis for distinguishing emotional intelligence from personality traits [9]. Accordingly, Goleman [4] mixed almost all characteristics except IQ, and is evaluated as similar to personality characteristics. Also, compared to Salovey and Mayer [13], there is a difference in that the emphasis on the cognitive aspect of emotional intelligence is weak [19]. Therefore, although Goleman's concept contributed greatly to popularization, it has been criticized for obscuring the distinction from existing psychological variables by overly interpreting emotional intelligence as motivation or personality type.

Meanwhile, research on emotional intelligence is being conducted in Korea through various scholars. Representatively, Moon [11] conducted a study to derive characteristics of emotional intelligence suitable for Koreans by examining the components of emotional intelligence based on the emotional intelligence model presented by Salovey and Mayer [14]. Based on this, it was emphasized that emotional intelligence is not a simple psychological characteristic but an ability that operates as a cognitive processing process through conceptualization through each subdomain of emotional intelligence [9]. In addition, through this study, Moon Yong-Rin [20, 21] more clearly divided the sub-domains included in the components of emotional intelligence and modeled them into 16 elements in 4 areas and 4 levels. He also asserted that she establishes hierarchies and levels between these competencies and that each component constitutes an organizational structure (see **Table 2**).

Field		**Level**
Field I	Recognition and expression of emotions	[Level 1] Understanding one's own emotions [Level 2] Understanding emotions outside of oneself [Level 3] Express emotions accurately [Level 4] Distinguishing expressed emotions
Field II	Emotional thinking promotion	[Level 1] Prioritize thinking using emotional information [Level 2] Using emotions to judge and remember [Level 3] Taking various perspectives using emotions [Level 4] Utilizing emotion to facilitate problem solving
Field III	Use of emotional knowledge	[Level 1] Understanding and naming the relationship between subtle emotions [Level 2] Interpreting the meaning contained in emotion [Level 3] Understanding complex and complex emotions [Level 4] Understanding the transition between emotions
Field IV	Reflective regulation of emotions	[Level 1] Accepting both positive and negative emotions [Level 2] Keep a distance from your emotions or look reflectively [Level 3] Reflectively look into emotions in the relationship between oneself and others [Level 4] Control one's own and others' emotions

Source: Moon [21].

Table 2.
16-factor model of 4 domains and 4 levels of emotional intelligence.

Meanwhile, efforts are being made in Korea to specify the concept of emotional intelligence and prepare a theoretical framework [11, 17, 20]. Looking at the definitions of various scholars, Hwang, Lee, and Jeon [22] referred to the definitions of Mayer and Salovey [14] and found that the ability to evaluate and express one's own and others' emotions, the ability to effectively control one's own and others' emotions, It was defined as the ability to know how to use those emotions to plan and achieve one's life.

Kang and Ha [23] defined it as the ability to understand and express one's own emotions, to recognize and understand the emotions of others, and to efficiently utilize and control emotions. Han et al. [24] defined it as the ability to understand, control, and utilize the emotions of oneself and others in various situations based on the research of Wong and Law [16]. Based on the definition of Goleman [4], intelligence was defined as the ability to understand one's own emotions, the ability to regulate emotions, the ability to self-motivate through emotions, the ability to understand others' emotions, and the ability to control interpersonal relationships. It was defined as the ability to understand the emotions of oneself and others in situations, and to control and utilize one's own emotions.

Park [25] defined it as "the ability to recognize one's own emotions and adjust and utilize them in relationships with others and the ability to recognize the emotions of others and utilize them efficiently", Kim and Yang [26] defined it as "the ability of a learner to control and regulate emotions through understanding their own emotions, and to express and adapt emotions well in a given situation to smoothly solve interpersonal problems."

In a similar context, Kim [27] reviewed the concept of emotional intelligence and analyzed the application of emotional intelligence to educational situations. Through this study, Kim [27] identified emotional intelligence as the ability to perceive emotions, induce and evaluate emotions to support thinking, the ability to grasp the meaning of one's own emotions related to general emotions, and good emotions. It was defined as the ability to regulate emotions that lead to thinking. In addition, he suggested that the study of emotional intelligence and learners' academic achievement and social performance would be an important task in the future.

In addition, Lee and Lee [28] conceptualized four factors: emotional perception, emotional thinking promotion, emotional understanding, and emotional regulation based on the emotional intelligence system presented by Salovey and Mayer [14]. They developed an emotional intelligence scale for young children through research trends in emotional intelligence. Through this, it was found that the emotional intelligence score increased as the child's age increased. In addition, it was emphasized that the sub-factor of emotional intelligence is emotional ability, which is different from the mixed model that approaches personality traits.

In addition, studies that conceptualized the definition of emotional intelligence based on the competency model of Salovey and Mayer [14] are as follows. First, Jung and Kim [29] conceptualized emotional intelligence as emotional evaluation and expression of oneself and others, emotional regulation, and emotional utilization. Lee and Jeong [30] defined it as the ability to understand and control the emotions of oneself and others as a positive emotional tendency possessed by humans. Park [25] viewed her ability to recognize her own emotions in her relationships with others, and to control and utilize them. In addition, Hwang and his colleagues [22], and Kim and Kim [31] defined various concepts and factors constituting it.

On the other hand, research on emotional intelligence was also conducted, focusing on the mixed model. Representatively, through the relationship between emotional intelligence and career decision-making self-efficacy, Yoo and Lee [32] confirmed the important role of emotional intelligence in career decision-making self-efficacy of college students. Based on this, they defined emotional intelligence as the ability to accurately perceive and recognize other people's emotions and express them appropriately, the ability to effectively adjust emotions to improve one's life, and the ability to pursue goals through motivation [32]. Through this, the sub-elements of self-emotional recognition, self-emotional regulation, self-motivation, recognition of others' emotions, and interpersonal relationship suggested by Goleman [4] were presented.

In addition, there are studies that have analyzed the concept and components of emotional intelligence by combining the competency model and the mixed model. First, Lee and Lee [33] presented various evidence on the reliability and validity of the Trait Meta-Mood Scale (TMMS) developed by Salovey et al. [34]. Through this, they found that the sub-factors of TMMS were excellent, and through this, Salovey and Mayer's emotional intelligence theory was valid. It was conceptualized as the degree to which one pays attention to one's feelings, the degree to which one clearly experiences such feelings, and the degree of belief that can end a negative emotional state and sustain a positive emotional state. In addition, Kim and Kim [2] developed an emotional intelligence scale for teachers that can be used in the field of early childhood education based on the emotional intelligence of Salovey and Mayer [13] and Goleman [4]. Accordingly, they suggested six factors, including self-emotional use, others' emotional awareness, self-emotional awareness, emotional regulation and impulse suppression, relationship with teacher, and relationship with peers, in consideration of developmental characteristics of young children.

Summarizing the above, it can be confirmed that most domestic studies conceptualize emotional intelligence based on Salovey and Mayer's [13] emotional intelligence theory and Goleman's [4] emotional intelligence theory. However, in the case of the mixed model applying Goleman's [4] emotional intelligence theory, it has been consistently argued that it is difficult to distinguish the concept of emotional intelligence from other concepts, including not only emotional abilities but also other personal characteristics [1, 10, 35, 36]. This is because the cognitive aspect, a key factor, may be overlooked due to the extended interpretation of emotional intelligence [37].

2.3 Emotional intelligence' related variables and studies

In general, emotions are known to have a positive effect on creativity [38]. Because joy, relaxation, laughter, and enthusiasm have a positive effect on creativity, stable emotions are a precursor to creativity. In particular, intrinsic motivation is important for the expression of creativity [39], and positive emotions promote divergent thinking. Therefore, emotional disorders can be an obstacle to creativity. Radford [40] said that the effectiveness of creativity depends on emotion. Creativity is a complex information processing process within a special concept. At this time, emotions effectively guide creativity by simplifying or removing certain information or inducing other intuitive information by unconsciously performing emotional reflection [41].

In addition, Radford said that when creativity, a complex information processing process, challenges the realm of perception, there is a risk of falling into reckless danger, and what can guide creativity at this time is a high level of emotional harmony. Creativity should be guided by being assimilated with emotion. Averill and Nualley [42] newly defined the term emotional creativity by linking emotion and creativity [38]. Emotional creativity, based on the perspective of social constructivism, means to refine, and express emotion in a new and unique way, away from traditional and standard methods.

Therefore, emotion can be a creative result by a new and unique way of expressing oneself. Therefore, it can be seen that emotion interacts with divergent thinking and leads to innovative thinking and re-creation [43]. In addition, emotional disorders, intrinsic motivation, emotional reflection, emotional coordination, and high-level expression of emotions mentioned above are all linked to emotional intelligence [41].

In particular, Morgan, Ponticell, and Gordon [44] said that creativity education programs should be applied as emotional education programs, and emotional education means emotional intelligence. Given the many theoretical claims that emotional intelligence has a positive effect on creativity [45]. The theoretical relationship between emotional intelligence and creativity has been proven through empirical research.

Academic achievement is the degree to which educational goals have been achieved through teaching and learning. Academic achievement is made up of interactions among learners, professors, and environmental variables, but IQ has been mentioned as an important factor [46]. However, emotional intelligence has recently been identified as an important variable affecting academic achievement. Although high-intensity emotions can interfere with cognitive processes, it is generally suggested that emotion affects cognition of complex and ambiguous tasks [47] and plays a key role in neurological thinking and judgment [4]. Also, ability emotional intelligence is mentioned as having a close relationship with school dropout as well as academic outcomes. Therefore, the factor of emotional intelligence must be introduced into the curriculum, and there must be a customized program linking academic and emotional intelligence [48], and emotional intelligence in the area of academic achievement evaluation. Empirical studies are also being presented in Korea. It was suggested that Salovey and Mayer's emotional intelligence [20] had a significant correlation with academic achievement [41].

Park et al. [49] reports that emotional intelligence is effective for school adjustment of specialized vocational high school students. Cho [50] found that the gifted students with high emotional appraisal and emotional regulation abilities felt less stress in their school lives. He also showed gifted students' emotional appraisal and emotional utilization were important predictors for their employment of more adaptive stress coping behaviors including problem solving and seeking for support. All these results were interpreted to suggest for the need to promote for improving the aspects of emotional intelligence in order to help the gifted students get adjusted more fully to their school lives.

Jun and Jung [5] analyzed the emotional status of college students in South Korea by gender and economic life level and suggested. The mean of positive psychological factors

Classification	Variables	No.	Minimum score	Maximum score	Mean	SD
Positive emotions	Self-esteem	1220	1.40	4.00	2.95	.43
	Ego-resilience	1220	1.50	4.00	2.84	.38
	Self-identity	1220	1.38	4.00	2.67	.40
	Life satisfaction	1220	1.00	4.00	2.85	.55
Negative emotions	Attention deficit	1220	1.00	3.71	2.05	.50
	Aggression	1220	1.00	3.67	1.78	.51
	Depression	1220	1.00	3.70	1.81	.52
	Social withdrawal	1220	1.00	4.00	2.20	.70

Table 3.
Descriptive statistics of emotional variables of college students.

(M = 2.83) was higher than that of negative psychological factors (M = 1.96). In positive psychological factors, self-esteem with a value of 2.95 was the highest, followed by life satisfaction with 2.85, ego-resilience with 2.84, and self-identity with 2.67. In negative psychological factors, social withdrawal with a score of 2.20 was the highest, followed by attention deficit with 2.05, depression with 1.81, and aggression with 1.78 (**Table 3**).

3. Discussions and conclusions

Emotional intelligence is gaining importance as a new concept for strengthening students' character in the critical consciousness of fostering selfish talent in the Korean society where competition for entrance exams is fierce. In Korea, emotional intelligence is based on the concept and components proposed by John Mayer and Peter Salovey [14], and the model proposed by Professor Moon Yong-Rin [9]. Therefore, it can be said that in Korea, the competency and cognitive model of emotional intelligence are mostly accepted rather than the mixed model based on Goleman [4]. In the case of the mixed model applying Goleman's [4] emotional intelligence theory, it has been consistently argued that it is difficult to distinguish the concept of emotional intelligence from other concepts, including not only emotional abilities but also other personal characteristics [36].

Most of the Korean tools for measuring emotional intelligence, as well as the concept of emotional intelligence, are translations of foreign scales. In Korea, Moon Yong-rin's scale is most commonly used, which is also based on Peter and Salovy's scale. Moon Yong-rin's scale is modified and used according to the research subjects, such as infants, elementary school students, middle school students, high school students, college students, and adults, so it is necessary to develop a specialized emotional intelligence scale for each subject.

Choi Hae-yeon and Choi Jong-an [51] extracted factors of positive and negative emotions, focusing on key keywords that can express Korean emotions according to the need to understand the emotional structure of Koreans. As a result of factor analysis of emotional experience report data of 250 college students and office workers, five positive emotions "affection", "achievement", "amusement", "relaxedness", and "gratitude" were extracted, whereas negative emotion consisted of seven factors, such as "sadness", "anger", "anxiety", "jealousy", "guilty", "boredom", and "unclassified distress". As such, it is hoped that studies on Korean emotions and their measurement will be conducted more actively in the future so that the unique emotional structure of Koreans can be identified and such emotional intelligence can be measured.

Author details

Soo-Koung Jun[1*] and Sook Hee Ryue[2]

1 Namseoul University, Cheonan, South Korea

2 Multiple Intelligence Institute, Seoul, South Korea

*Address all correspondence to: skjun74@hanmail.net

References

[1] Jung OB, Jung SH, Lim JH. Emotional Development and Emotional Intelligence. Seoul: Hakjisa; 2018

[2] Kim KH, Kim KH. A study on construct validation of emotional intelligence in young children. Journal of the Korean Psychological Development Association. 1999;**12**(1):25-38

[3] Moon YR, Kwak YJ. A longitudinal study of the relationship between emotional intelligence and position. Human Development Research. 2005;**12**(4):19-31

[4] Goleman D. Emotional Intelligence. New York: Bantam Books; 1995

[5] Jun SK, Jung IS. Exploration of the differences in positive-negative psychological factors influencing the life satisfaction and depression of college students by gender and family economic level. International Journal of Advanced and Applied Sciences. 2022;**9**(4):88-96

[6] Lee MR, Park BH. Development and validation of school life burnout progress scale for college students. Educational Psychology Research. 2018;**32**(2):229-247

[7] Jang DY, Kang YB. The effect of college students' perception of family health on career adaptability: Mediating effect of emotional intelligence. Youth Facility Environment. 2019;**17**(1):59-70

[8] Ha MS. Relationship among 5 personality factors of college students, emotional intelligence, depression, and aggression. Study on Self-centered Learning Subject Matter Education. 2017;**17**(17):197-222

[9] Moon YR. Intelligence and Education. Seoul: Hakjisa; 2013

[10] Moon YR, Kang MS, Choi KH. Validation study of EQ life attitude test. Human Development Research. 2004;**11**(3):1-16

[11] Moon YR. The present and future of emotional intelligence research. Journal of the Korean Society of Children's Studies. 1998;**12**:1-16

[12] Ryue SH. Multi-Intelligence Forest Program. Pajoo: Korea Academic Information Service; 2008

[13] Mayer JD, Salovey P. Emotional Intelligence. Imagination, Cognition, and Personality. 1990;**9**:185-211

[14] Mayer JD, Salovey P. What is emotional intelligence? In: Salovey P, Sluyter D, editors. Emotional Development and Emotional Intelligence: Educational Implications. New York: Basic Books; 1997. pp. 3-31

[15] Bar-On R. The Emotional Quotient Inventory (EQ-1):Technical Manual. Toronto, Canada: Multi-Health Systems; 1997. p. 1997

[16] Wong CS, Law KS. The effects of leader and follower emotional intelligence on performance and attitude: An exploratory study. The Leadership Quarterly. 2002;**13**(3):243-274

[17] Moon YR. A study on emotional intelligence development programs in schools. Seoul National University College of Education. 2001;**62**:27-53

[18] Sunindijo RY, Hadikusumo BH, Ogunlana S. Emotional intelligence and leadership styles in construction project management. Journal of management in engineering. 2007;**23**(4):166-170

[19] Lee KM, Lim W. A study on the job validity of emotional intelligence for the

development of educational programs based on emotional intelligence. Educational Method Research. 2016;**28**(3):587-608

[20] Moon YR. EQ Diary: Samsung Human Resources Development Center New Employee Training Program. Seoul: Samsung Human Resources Development Institute; 1997

[21] Moon YR. MI Aptitude Career Test. Seoul: Daekyo Korean Education Evaluation Center; 2003

[22] Hwang PJ, Lee IS, Jeon MK. The effects of emotional intelligence of organizational members on job satisfaction and organizational citizenship behavior. Productivity Journal. 2011;**25**(3):311-330

[23] Kang JG, Ha DH. The effect of supervisor's emotional intelligence on the supervisor's transformational leadership and team performance in the hotel industry. Tourism Research. 2014;**29**(1):241-264

[24] Han GW, Choi WS, Na HK. The effect of customer-related stress on emotional labor: The moderating effect of emotional intelligence perceived by hotel workers. Korea Tourism Industry Association. 2016;**41**(2):193-218

[25] Park MJ. The effect of emotional intelligence on job performance of local children's center workers: Focusing on the mediating effect of organizational commitment. Education and Culture Research. 2019;**25**(2):379-398

[26] Kim KC, Yang AK. The effects of emotional intelligence and achievement motivation on self-directed learning in freshmen college students. Marine Education Research. 2019;**31**(2):574-585

[27] Kim YR. Analysis of the concept of emotional intelligence and its limitations in educational application. Journal of Education Research. 1999;**16**:3-24

[28] Lee SE, Lee YS. Development and validation of emotional intelligence scale for children. Pedagogical Research. 2004;**42**(3):519-551

[29] Jung HW, Kim CH. The effects of organizational members' emotional intelligence on organizational citizenship behavior: Moderating effect of LMX. Human Resource Management Research. 2007;**14**(3):167-186

[30] Lee SH, Jeong GY. A study on the relationship between emotional intelligence, communication competency and problem-solving ability of beauty-related college students. Management Education Research. 2018;**33**(2):51-78

[31] Kim JW, Kim BS. The relationship between emotional intelligence and mindfulness and career seeking behavior in college students. Research on Learner-centered Subject Education. 2018;**18**(6):849-867

[32] Yu NH, Lee KH. Differences in career decision-making self-efficacy according to attachment, psychological independence, and emotional intelligence. Korean Journal of Psychology: Counseling and Psychotherapy. 2005;**17**(2):451-466

[33] Lee SJ, Lee HG. A study on the validity of the trait meta-mood scale: Exploration of sub-factors of emotional intelligence. Journal of the Korean Psychological Association: Society and Personality. 1997;**11**(1):95-116

[34] Mayer JD, Salovey P, Goldman SL, Turvey C, Palfai TP. Emotional attention, clarity, and repair: Exploring emotional intelligence using the trait meta-mood scale. In: Penne-baker J, editor. Emotion, Disclosure, and Health. Washington, DC:

American Psychological Association; 1995. pp. 125-154p

[35] Gardner H. Who owns intelligence. The Atlantic Monthly. 1999;**283**(2):67-76

[36] Sternberg RJ, Review of D. Goleman's book working with emotional intelligence. Personnel Psychology. 1999;**52**:780-783

[37] Lee MS. Development and validation of emotional intelligence scale for college students. Learning Self-centered Subject Matter Education Research. 2020;**20**(17):903-935

[38] Averill JR. Intelligence, emotion, and creativity: From trichotomy to trinity. In: Bar-On R, Parker JDS, editors. The Handbook of Emotional Intelligence: Theory, Development, Assessment, and Application at Home, School, and in the Workplace. San Francisco: Jossey-Bass; 2000. pp. 277-298

[39] Urban KK. Creativity: A componential approach. In: Paper Presented at the 11th World Conference on Gifted and Talented Children, Hongkong, China. July 1995

[40] Radford M. Emotion and creativity. The Journal of Aesthetic Education. 2004;**38**(1):53-64

[41] Oh SY. Study on the relationship among emotional intelligence, leadership, creativity, and achievement [doctoral dissertation]. Seoul: Korea National University; 2018

[42] Averill JR, Nunley EP. Voyagers of the Heart: Living an Emotionally Creative Life. New York: The Free Press; 1992

[43] Scott SG, Bruce RA. Determinant of innovative behavior: A path model of individual innovation in workplace. Academy of Management Journal. 1994;**37**:580-607

[44] Morgan R, Ponticell J, Gordon A. Rethinking Creativity. Washingto, D. C.: Fast back; 2000

[45] Burch GSJ. Creativity and emotional intelligence. Selection and Development Review. 2003;**19**(2):3-6

[46] Roedel TD, Schraw G. Belief about intelligence and academic goals. Contemporary Educational Psychology. 1995;**20**(4):464-468

[47] Forgas JP. Mood and judgement: The affect infusion model (AIM). Psychological Bulletin. 1995;**117**:39-66

[48] Maree J, Eiselen RJ. The emotional intelligence profile of academics in merger setting. Education and Urban Society. 2004;**36**(4):482-504

[49] Park SH, Song GW, Lee CH. The effect of emotional intelligence on school adjustment of specialized vocational high school students. Journal of the Korean Society of Industrial Education. 2018;**43**(1):41-57

[50] Cho HC. Relations between gifted students' emotional intelligence and their social skills, school adjustment, stress and stress coping strategies. Gifted children and Gifted Education. 2010;**9**(1):121-140

[51] Choi HY, Choi JA. The structure and measurement of Koreans' emotion. Korean Journal of Social and Personality Psychology. 2016;**30**(2):89-114

Chapter 6

Emotion Recognition – Recent Advances and Applications in Consumer Behavior and Food Sciences with an Emphasis on Facial Expressions

Udo Wagner, Klaus Dürrschmid and Sandra Pauser

Abstract

For decades, the study of emotions has been the center of attention in research and practice. Based on relevant literature, this paper focuses on the subject of measurement, and provides a structured overview of common measurement tools by distinguishing between methods of communication and observation. Given the authors' field of competence, presentation pursues a consumer behavior and food sciences perspective. Furthermore, the paper devotes attention to automatic facial expressions analysis technology which advanced considerably in recent years. Three original empirical examples from the authors' range of experience reveal strengths and weaknesses of this technology.

Keywords: emotions, measurement, facial expressions, emotion recognition, consumer behavior

1. Introduction

1.1 Intended contribution

For decades, emotions have been a hot topic in multiple scientific disciplines such as Psychology (cf. the seminal work of Darwin published first in 1872). They are said to be an integral part of human nature while contributing to behavior control but were sometimes thought to bias rational thinking and behavior. Theories on the study of emotions are manifold. For example, Scherer's ([1], p. 697) view is very broad in that he defines emotions as an "episode of interrelated, synchronized changes in the states of all [...] organismic subsystems in response to the evaluation of an external or internal stimulus." Consequently, his *component process model* of emotions indicates a comprehensive conception by pointing to the organismic human subsystems (central nervous system, neuro-endocrine system, autonomic nervous system, and somatic nervous system) which become active in response to the evaluation of occurring stimuli and induce an emotion in turn: (i) cognitive component (appraisal); (ii) neurophysiological component (bodily symptoms, arousal); (iii) motivational component (action tendencies); (iv) motor expression component (facial and vocal expression); and (v) subjective feeling component (emotional experience). In an ideal world of science, the researcher would need to measure all components. However, Scherer ([1], p. 709) concedes that "comprehensive measurement of emotion has never been performed and is unlikely to become standard procedure in the near future."

Whereas Scherer's [1] component process model provides a thorough and multifacet view on emotions, this chapter—while focusing on measurement issues—pays tribute to practicability. As discussed later, measurement procedures employed empirically, typically focus on a single aspect of emotions only. Given this view, this paper intends to provide a structured overview of common tools that enable the measurement of emotions. Furthermore, the focus lies on measurement procedures in consumer behavior and food science. In particular, special attention is devoted to automatic facial expressions analysis technology which advanced considerably in recent years.

The remainder of this book chapter is structured as follows. The next subsection provides a theoretical foundation from the literature which delivers insights into the concepts of emotional measurement procedures. Section 2 is central for this chapter and presents a variety of means for measuring emotions. It is structured according to methods of communication and of observation. Section 3 offers three empirical examples that employ automatic facial expressions analysis technology for capturing customers' emotions while being exposed to commercials or tasting food products. These examples underpin the strengths and weaknesses of the employed means of technology. Section 4 concludes by providing recommendations for research and practice.

1.2 Basic considerations on emotions

The *classical* view on emotions is a categorical and dimensional theory. It claims that only a limited number of basic emotions exist. These emotions, in turn, are described as inborn reactions that universally apply to all cultures [2, 3]. Ekman and colleagues suggested that facial expressions (cf. a motor expression component of emotions) can be categorized into a small number of basic emotions like happiness, fear, anger, surprise, disgust, contempt, and sadness. The theory of *constructed emotions* offers a different point of view [4, 5] and contradicts the classical view in many aspects: First, emotions are not inborn reactions, but arise from basic components. Second, emotions are not universal, but vary from culture to culture. Third, they are not triggered, but are expressed by the individual. Fourth, emotions emerge as a combination of the physical properties of the body, a flexible brain that wires itself to any environment it develops in, and the culture and education, which form that environment.

Consensus exists that emotions are the results of certain stimuli that do not last very long as compared to feelings. Thus, emotions are often considered as "short-term affective responses to the appraisal of particular stimuli" ([6], p. 191). In relation to that, the *appraisal theory* claims that emotions are elicited when an event is being evaluated, which contributes to an important goal of the individual [7–9]. The connotation of the emotion is positive when the concern is advanced and negative when the concern is impeded. This theory is in line with Rolls' [10] conceptualization which defines emotions as states elicited by rewards and punishments. In this sense, emotions regulate distance and nearness. For example, the emotion of disgust elicits avoidance behaviors (distance), while positive emotions such as happiness promote approach behaviors (nearness). According to Gibson ([11], p. 54), feelings last in contrast to emotions longer and are referred to as psychological arousal states with "interacting dimensions related to energy, tension and pleasure (hedonic tone) [...] and may be more covert to observers". (Sources: Matthews & Deary, 1998; Rolls, 2007).

The *appraisal theory* follows a cognitive approach and focuses on the mind's organization of conscious and unconscious knowledge, and on the fundamental questions of how emotions are caused and what their effects are. Oatley and Johnson-Laird [12] describe three cognitive theories of emotion: (1) the *action-readiness theory*, (2) the *core-affect theory*, and (3) the *communicative theory*. Ad (1), the action-readiness theory holds that emotions are built from elements that are not itself emotions. Frijda and Parrott [13] label them as "basic emotions," viewed as states of readiness for certain actions, giving priority to a particular goal. Ad (2), the core-affect theory postulates two stages in generating an emotion: level of arousal and valence level (pleasure–displeasure) [1, 14]. Ad (3), the communicative theory claims that emotions relate to communication within the brain and amongst individuals [9] and that distinct basic emotions have evolved as adaptations in social mammals.

Another important consideration is whether emotions are conscious or unconscious by nature. One stream of literature describes an emotion as the conscious subjective experience that accompanies affective states created by bodily sensations [6, 15]. However, several more recent studies point to the existence of unconscious emotions. In particular, a person is not aware of these emotions when explicitly asked to report them [16].

James [17] and Lange [18] represent the premise that emotional experiences are produced by sensing peripheral bodily changes like heart rate or tensions in the skeletal muscles, which are referred to as somatic markers [19]. This leads to the—for many contra-intuitive—situation, that an individual is not running away, because (s)he is scared, but rather is scared because of (s)he is running away. Many objections have been raised against this theory, which are summarized by Rolls [10].

In conclusion, emotions appear on at least three dimensions. First, they are experienced by individuals in a distinct subjective manner. This is the most common and widely known aspect of emotions—everybody knows, how disgust, sadness or happiness, etc. feel. Second, emotions are often connected with changes in physiology, mainly in reactions of the autonomic nervous system. Sweating or perceiving a strange stomach/gut feeling are two examples for physiological reactions. Third, emotions have a behavioral aspect, which means that emotions can change the behavior of an individual such as facial expressions, posture, walking speed, speech, or gestures [20, 21]. Irrespective of the question, which of these dimensions appears first, second, and last, and how they interact, these three dimensions can be used and have been used (subjective experience, physiology, and behavior) to characterize the emotional state of an individual.

2. Selected measures of emotions

Table 1 provides a structured overview of the most appropriate measurement approaches developed in the last decades (see for instance Coppin and Sander [22] for an alternative survey). On the *first level*, we distinguish whether these methods employ communication or observational techniques (upper or lower panel of **Table 1**).

Means of communication		
Degree of structure	Degree of disguise	
	Undisguised	Disguised
Unstructured	Personal interviews	Content analysis of diaries
	Think-aloud technique	Associative networks
		Zaltman metaphor elicitation technique (ZMET)
Structured	Verbal scales	Picture / photo scale
	Differential Emotions Scale (DES)	Self-Assessment Manikin Technique (SAM)
	Pleasure/Arousal/Dominance scale (PAD)	PrEmo-instrument ©
	Emotions Profile Index (EPI)	EmoSensor
	Positive And Negative Affect Schedule (PANAS)	Emotive Projection Test (EPT)
	Consumption Emotion Set (CES)	Implicit Association Test (IAT)
	Temporal Dominance of Sensations (TDS)	
	EsSense Profile ®	
Means of observation		
Method of administration	Setting	
	Contrived laboratory setting	Near-to-life/real-life setting
Human	Facial expressions (FAST, FACS)	Facial expressions (FAST, FACS)
	Body movements	Body movements
		Mystery shopping
Technical equipment	Facial ElectrocMyoGraphy (fEMG)	Voice pitch analysis
	Automatic Facial Expressions Analysis (AFEA)	Automatic Facial Expressions Analysis (AFEA)
	Electro Dermal Response (EDR)	Neurophysiological measures using wearables (EDR, pupillary dilation, heart rate)
	Electro EncephaloGraphy (EEG), Positron Emission Tomography (PET), functional Magnetic Resonance Imaging (fMRI)	
	Program analyzer	

Table 1.
Overview of emotional measurement procedures.

When using means of communication, subjects provide information about their emotional experience verbally in their own words or by responding to scales or by commenting on pictures or photographs. Clearly, this is a conscious process. These methods are therefore based on introspection and self-reports.

Observational techniques have been employed or developed to avoid possible biases of introspection-based self-reports (i.e., social-desirable response behavior). Observations can be used in an implicit way, which means that the measurement outcomes reflect the construct under investigation (e.g., emotions) in an automatic manner based on processes that are uncontrolled, unintentional, goal-independent, purely stimulus-driven, autonomous, unconscious, efficient, and fast. Physiological, neurological, and behavioral reactions deliver implicit measures, in contrast to explicit measures, which are controlled, intentional, goal-dependent, not only stimulus-driven, conscious, slow, and potentially intrusive [23]. Data from implicit measures are said to have more external validity and therefore, contribute more to the understanding and prediction of human behavior in real life.

Dijksterhuis [24] suggests three criteria for the evaluation of the implicitness of a method. Does the subject (1) need to think about him−/herself to answer; (2) know that (s)he is tested; (3) know about the research question? The more yes-answers are provided the less implicit, the more no-answers are stated the more implicit the evaluated method is. Columns of **Table 1** (reflecting the *second level* of classification) refer to the latter by distinguishing between degrees of disguise, setting, respectively. Typically, subjects are neither informed about the research agenda nor are always aware of the conducted study in a disguised or real-life setting (such a situation would be called probiotic). Ethical issues concerning research integrity have to be considered in such cases to a great extent, but these considerations are beyond the scope of this article.

The *third level* (rows of **Table 1**) categorizes measures of emotions according to a more technical aspect degree of structure (i.e., degree of standardization imposed on the questions asked and the answers permitted) or the method of administration (human vs. technical equipment).

2.1 Methods using means of communication

All methods employing means of communication use the ability of humans for introspection, and reporting about the result of introspection, such as emotions in terms of language, pictures, or photos. Implicitly they are thus following (some variant of) appraisal theory. Scholars favoring, for example, a biologic theory, accentuate limitations referred to as cognitive bias inherent in self-report measures. There are enormous differences in the test design on how individuals are enabled to communicate the results of their introspection. As an aside, qualitative methods introduced in the following two subsections have been adapted for emotion measurement but were originally developed for a broader spectrum.

2.1.1 Unstructured, undisguised communication methods

Personal interviews The personal interview, with a more or less structured conversation, is led by an instructed interviewer. Within a free-response format, the researcher asks participants to respond with freely chosen labels or short expressions that best characterize the nature of the emotional state they experience when being confronted with a certain external or internal stimulus (cf. [1]). A guideline helps to lead the interview. Personal interviews score highly with respect to flexibility but negatively on issues such as the subjects' potential problems communicating personal responses with appropriate expressions, individual differences in the range of their active vocabulary, and biasing influences of the interviewer on the communication process. In addition, the recruiting of subjects might be challenging since the process needs to be executed (and recorded) in a quiet surrounding and takes a considerable amount of time. Making the data amenable to quantitative analysis requires categorization which is a labor-intensive process. Scherer [1] offers the Geneva Affect Label Coder (GALC) which attempts to recognize 36 affective categories commonly distinguished by words in natural language.

Think-aloud technique Subjects are asked to perform a specific task (for the present situation for instance looking at a certain video clip or website; walking through a store and finding a certain product on the shelf; tasting a certain meal) and to articulate whatever comes into their mind (in particular their perceived feelings and emotions) as they complete the task. These verbalizations of subjects' cognitive processes are recorded by the researcher (if present) or on a technical device (e.g., a voice recorder) and its content is analyzed thereafter. We emphasize the dynamic component of this method because protocols have to be connected with the various stages and aspects of the task to find out which particular emotions they elicited at which point in time.

2.1.2 Unstructured, disguised communication methods

Content analysis of diaries Traditionally, diary studies request subjects to self-report certain behaviors or activities over a longer period of time which seems to contradict the definition of emotions as a short episode in time (i.e., contrasting feelings, cf. subsection 1.2). A special format of diaries [25], event-based diaries or in-situ loggings, asks participants to log information in the situation they occur. The situation in turn is defined by the researcher as an event (e.g., consuming a certain product), a usage scenario (e.g., engaging with a certain product), or making a selfie in a certain location, searching for photographs about past events or consumption experiences, etc. To emphasize the short-term characteristic of emotions, reporting might be executed by audio/video devices, hand-held computers, or means of social media rather than by traditional paper diaries. Spontaneity of responses is important to mitigate potential rationalization. The interpretation of reports requires diligent (content) analysis.

Associative networks This method [26] builds upon the well-established theory that human memory might be viewed at as possessing a network structure consisting of nodes (representing stored information of an object) and interconnecting links (representing the strength of the association between thereby connected objects). For the present case, the researcher is interested in the arousing potential of a stimulus (e.g., an ad, a food product) on different emotions (e.g., surprise). Thus, when using this technique, free associations with stimulus words or stimulus images are entered on a sheet of paper in a list. By entering the list, the order (and the spontaneity) of the associations is automatically recorded. After that, subjects evaluate the recorded words in another column of this sheet of paper (as having a negative, neutral or positive meaning in the considered context). In the next step, subjects are asked to assign as many as possible of the previously recorded words to already predefined categories. This has the advantage that the categorization does not have to be carried out subsequently by the researcher. The categorization scheme has to be developed within a pre-study or existing schemes (e.g., GALC) might be adopted for the present application.

ZMET Zaltman Metaphor Elicitation Technique [27] is a patented technique of marketing research, which aims at determining conscious and unconscious thoughts, feelings, and emotions by investigating the symbolic and metaphorical answers of the tested individuals. Starting point of this technique is the collection of pictures that represent the thoughts and emotions of a study participant at their premises. These pictures help to discover the often-unconscious thoughts and feelings, whose structure is investigated in the following interviews. In essence, it is a sophisticated combination of an event-based diary (collection of pictures at the subjects' home), an in-depth personal interview (at the researcher's lab) conceptually based on neural network brain structures.

2.1.3 Structured, undisguised communication methods

There is a huge variety of scales intending to measure emotions. We restrict our presentation to a few starting with scales conceptualized for general, rather than psychological, purposes; DES might be classified as a discrete emotions approach, PAD, EPI, PANAS as dimensional approaches. Subsequently, we provide three scales which are targeting consumer behavior (CES), food sciences (TDS, EsSense Profile ®).

DES The main idea behind Izard's [28] Differential Emotions Scale rests on the existence of 10 basic emotions and the assumption that language-based categories correspond to unique emotion-specific patterns (cf. action-readiness theory). Thirty items comprise the DES: three adjectives per basic emotion (e.g., for anger "enraged," "angry," and "mad"). Respondents are asked to describe their emotional state by (dis) approving to each item on a rating scale. These ratings are then aggregated yielding a score per basic emotion.

PAD Mehrabian and Russell [29] are pioneers in the field of environmental psychology. They propose a SIR (stimulus–intervening processes–response) model of consumer behavior in which *emotional* (intervening) variables play an important role. Based on previous work, they suggest describing emotions by their position in a three-dimensional space formed by the dimensions of Pleasure, Arousal, and Dominance. They develop a scale with six items for each dimension. The items are framed as a semantic differential (e.g., "happy/unhappy" for pleasure).

EPI The dominance dimension of the PAD is criticized by scholars, amongst others because of the lack of empirical support for this construct (and practicability issues as a three-dimensional space is difficult to present in a two-dimensional figure). Many theorists, therefore, limit their models to the two dimensions of valence and arousal (slightly renaming the pleasure dimension; cf. core-effect theory). Plutchik's [30] Emotions Profile Index is representative for these approaches. This profile consists of 62 pairs of properties (e.g., "affectionate vs. cautious") and subjects are asked to choose which of the two alternatives applies for them. Finally, responses are aggregated and represented in a circumplex, which is conceptually very similar to his wheel of emotions (with eight basic emotions and three different levels of intensity). As an example, opposing emotions are displayed at opposing positions of the circumplex, like joy versus sadness (assumed to possess opposing valence but similar arousal). Scherer's [1] Geneva Emotion Wheel is conceptually very similar but with two exceptions: he proposes 16 basic emotions arranged according to the dimensions' conduciveness and coping potential. In fact, it turns out, that changing dimensions corresponds to a 45° rotation of the axes of the circumplex.

PANAS The Positive And Negative Affects Schedule [31] can also be viewed as a dimensional approach, however, these dimensions are not related to the constructs from above. The dimensions only distinguish between positive and negative emotions. Each dimension is described by 10 adjectives (e.g., "active" for the positive, "afraid" for then negative dimension) and Likert-framed response categories.

CES Based on extant literature and in particular, extensive empirical studies, Richins [32] developed the Consumption Emotion Set. Conceptually it is similar to the

DES but adopted to the purpose of consumption-related emotions. The scale encompasses 17 different categories with two or three descriptors each (e.g., for anger "frustrated," "angry," and "irritated"), in sum 47 items with a rating response format.

TDS Jager et al. [33] adopted the Temporal Dominance of Sensation method to emotions, which is intended to measure the *dynamics* of food-related emotions during consumption. They use 10 emotional attributes and participants have to rate the dominance of these 10 emotions while eating. For instance, in the case of chocolate, this method results in the temporal description of emotions elicited by the experience of chocolate during oral processing. In the first seconds "interested" might be dominant, followed by the emotions "energetic" and "happy," in the end also "loving," "calm," and "guilty" might be found dominant.

EsSense Profile ® Literature originating from the field of (clinical) Psychology is particularly interested in negatively valenced emotions (corresponding with some psychical illness). The circumplex model implicitly implies some symmetry between positively and negatively valenced emotions (as does, e.g., the PANAS scales with 10 items each). Naturally, in a consumption context, positive emotions play a more important role. The EsSense Profile ® (King and Meiselmann [34]) pays tribute to this focus: the profile consists of 25 positive (e.g., "glad"), 3 negative (e.g., "bored"), and 11 unclear (e.g., "eager," "daring," "tame") items. Subjects describe their emotional state by (dis)approving to each item on a rating scale. Aggregated (over respondents) ratings are displayed in a radar chart or consolidated by multivariate techniques (factor or cluster analysis). EsSense Profile ® has been validated and gained influence in sensory science. In response to the critique regarding the scale (very subtle differences between the verbal emotion descriptions, which require high cognitive capabilities and articulateness from respondents), shorter versions of EsSense Profile ® have been proposed [35].

However, in all methods employing verbal scales it is certainly not clear whether the respondents' experienced emotions are measured or only their more or less vague associations with emotions elicited by the stimulus, which makes of course an enormous difference. Despite all reservations and problems of self-report questionnaires, Cardello and Jaeger [36] recommend scales as the default measuring method for emotions.

2.1.4 Structured, disguised communication methods

A general issue with verbal descriptions of emotions (as used in scales) is, that emotions are not always easily expressed with words and there also exist differences across cultures and languages in the emotion lexicon [5]. For that reason, alternative scales based on pictures rather than on verbal descriptors have been developed.

SAM Inspired by the PAD scale Lang [37] establishes the Self-Assessment Manikin scale which offers respondents visual response categories, that is, differently shaped pictograms. For the dimension pleasure, the "friendliness of the face" of the manikin is varied; for arousal indicated "body movements" and for dominance the "size" of the manikin. Positive experiences are reported in that subjects quickly complete and easily, intuitively and unambiguously understand the response format, however, some authors criticize the validity of this scale.

PrEmo-instrument © The Product Emotion Measurement Instrument [38] also employs visual response categories but these pictograms appear as a cartoon character and are not static but animated on a computer screen. Animation visualizes changing intensity of seven positive (desire, pleasant surprise, inspiration, amusement, admiration, satisfaction, fascination) or seven negative emotions (indignation, contempt, disgust, unpleasant surprise, dissatisfaction, disappointment, boredom). Gutjar et al. [39] apply PrEmo © in a food consumption context but the rather small number of emotions may not be sufficient for the description of the various emotions elicited by product categories like foods.

EmoSensor This scale, developed in cooperation between academics (Gröppel-Klein et al. [40]) and the market research institute GfK, offers photographs representing individuals (of different ages, gender, cultural provenience) engaged in different activities as visual response categories when asking respondents to assess their emotional response to a certain stimulus (for instance an ad). Verbal labeling attached to the photographs (e.g., joy) turned out to be advantageous. The scale consists of three photographs for each of the 22 different emotions. Subjects select the photo which best reflects their emotional state. The authors emphasize that facial expressions might be ambiguous in some cases and that, therefore, testing for reliability and validity was of crucial importance.

EPT The Emotive Projection Test is a special type of thematic apperception test (TAT). The TAT, also known as "picture interpretation technique," shows ambiguous scenes and by describing such scenes one can learn more about the participant's emotions, motivations, and personality. The EPT was developed by Köster, Mojet, and Van Veggel [41] and consists of 30 pictures with neutral or ambiguous facial expressions. When participants are asked to which state emotion is portrayed in each picture (using the "check all that apply" technique), they project their own emotions, moods, and feelings into the faces on the pictures. Participants ascribe characteristics to these faces that depend largely on their own emotions. Therefore, this test is an implicit (i.e., third person) test. It was used, for example, to study the effect of flowers on the mood of restaurant visitors [41] and the effect of vanilla in yogurt on emotional responses [42].

IAT One of the most often referenced tests in Psychology is the implicit association test, developed by Greenwald et al. [43]. Like the associative network concept, the IAT is based on the idea that the human brain is structured as a neural network with highly related content being more closely connected in this net than loosely connected content. Subjects have to solve a set of easy association tasks on a computer by pressing either of two answer-keys; their reaction time is recorded. Given the network structure of the brain, it is thus easier for participants to react with the same answer-key on associated elements than using the other key and therefore they are quicker in answering to associated elements than to not associated elements. Whereas the IAT was developed for general purposes (i.e., associations in memory), stimulus material shown on the screen can be adopted for the measurement of the emotional elicitation potential of a certain object.

2.2 Methods using means of observation

2.2.1 Observational methods with human administration in a laboratory setting

Facial expressions Emotions are communicated through facial expressions in everyday life [44] by non-verbal means [45]. Twenty face muscles create a wide array of facial expressions and muscles on the head allow meaningful movements of the jaw and neck [46]. Humans have the impression that the interpretation of facial expressions occurs mainly automatically, immediately and without any effort humans know what a certain facial expression means—joy, disgust, or surprise. In contrast, the objective description and quantification of facial expressions as emotions remain a difficulty.

Two general approaches exist to analyze facial expressions in an objective way, judgment- and anatomically-based methods [47]. Whereas for the former a coder directly classifies facial expressions as a certain emotion, for the latter (s)he measures the movement or activity of specific facial muscles and then relates the resulting activity pattern to the identified emotion. Human coders can be very accurate in judging facial reactions, both for anatomically as well as judgment approaches provided, that they are extensively trained. The analysis is considerably time-consuming and expensive.

In this context, Ekman and Friesen [48] developed the Facial Affect Scoring Technique (FAST), a judgment-based method, and the Facial Action Coding System (FACS), an anatomically based method. Since inspecting certain facial muscles thoroughly takes time, subjects' facial expressions are video recorded and their separate anatomical movements (i.e., "action units") are identified using a slow-motion playback of the video. The coding schemes assist in transferring the identified action units into related emotional expressions. Marketing applications analyzed, among others, facial expressions of customers at the point of sale, or when interacting with salespersons, or when being exposed to commercials.

Only few published studies make use of human coders to investigate emotions elicited by food. Zeinstra et al. [49] found that children's facial expressions, analyzed by human coders, are a good indication for disliking but not for liking of juices. Similarly, consumers showed more negative emotions just before tasting presumably insect-based chips compared to consumers who were expecting to taste protein enriched chips [50].

Body movements Body movements, including posture and gesture, can also be used as motor expressions of emotional states. Coding schemes (e.g., Berner System [51]) have been developed at about the same time as FAST and FACS. However, established relationships between bodily behaviors and emotions are less pronounced. Body movements are much more affected by culture, personal style, and context than facial expression. On the one hand, Weinberg [52] concludes that while facial expressions signal the type of emotional state, bodily expressions signal their intensity (e.g., a person who is feeling angry might gesture more forcefully, while a person who is feeling sad might gesture less). In a similar vein, individuals might more easily suppress or mask their true emotions with respect to facial expressiveness than with respect to body movements because they occur unconsciously to an even greater extent that facial movements. On the other hand, *exemplary* findings suggest that a person who is feeling confident might stand tall with their shoulders back, while a person who is feeling anxious might slouch or hunch their shoulders. In any case, the interpretation of body movements is highly complex and—to the best of the authors' knowledge—a comprehensive manual (with respect to emotional states) has not been developed so far and as a consequence, a software for automatic emotional pattern recognition based on bodily behaviors is missing.

2.2.2 Observational methods with human administration in a real-life setting

Facial expressions body movements For these methods, the setting does not make a substantial difference for measurement (and we thus refer to the previous subsection). In general, a laboratory setting better controls for environmental conditions and better recording, thus increasing internal validity, a real-life setting reduces or even excludes reactive behavior of subjects and increases external validity.

Mystery shopping Mystery shopping is rooted in ethnographic research and may be described as a special form of participating observation. In more detail, a trained individual, known as a mystery shopper, poses as a customer in order to evaluate the performance of a business [53]. Mystery shopping is not typically used for the purpose of measuring emotions but rather to evaluate customer service, sales, and other aspects (e.g., general attitudes of persons involved in an encounter) of a business' performance. To apply for emotion measurement, this individual needs to be trained in judgment-based expertise (see sub-Section 2.2.1) on relating facial or bodily expressions of customers and employees (e.g., during a sales or service interaction) to their emotional states. The short-term character of emotions, the unfeasibility of recording the interaction, and of taking notes limits the suitability of mystery shopping for emotion measurement.

2.2.3 Observational methods using technical equipment in a laboratory setting

fEMG The most direct and sensitive method to measure facial reactions is Facial ElectroMyoGraphy, where surface electrodes are attached to the face and the muscles' activities are amplified and displayed on a monitor [54]. Two face muscles are of special importance: the zygomaticus major (responsible for the expression of smiling) indicates positive valence and intensity of emotions, the corrugator (responsible for frowning) negative valence. A considerable limitation of fEMG is the application of electrodes to the face. This can be rather intrusive to the subject, it obviously limits the implicitness of the study and might bias results.

Applications are reported from fine arts but rarely from consumer behavior. For tasting food products or looking at pictures of food products, studies using fEMG have shown that the activity of selected facial muscles correlates with self-reported hedonic responses [55, 56].

AFEA Automatic Facial Expression Analysis systems have become widely available in the last decade. AFEA systems employ a software to automatically analyze facial reactions using judgment-based and anatomically approaches from video and image sources. In comparison to the use of trained human coders, this approach reduces time and costs of emotion investigations substantially.

Most AFEA systems conduct a similar 3-step strategy for the classification of facial expressions: (1) Face acquisition—identification of the face, its position, and orientation, (2) Feature extraction—two general approaches are used; either the whole face is processed holistically, or specific areas of the face are selected and processed individually. (3) Classification: based on a complex model, facial expressions are classified using either a direct classification of emotions or an anatomically based coding scheme (e.g., activation of muscles or muscle groups).[1] Furthermore, sophisticated algorithms (deep learning systems) take gender and age into account. In a laboratory setting, initial calibration of the measurement device adopted to the subjects to be observed might also account for cultural characteristics (e.g., facial expressions of East Asians); in a real-life setting, algorithms might identify such peculiarities instantaneously.

---

[1] The Robotics Institute of Carnegie Mellon University and University of Pittsburgh have been innovators in this area.

In marketing, AFEA has been applied in many different situation (e.g., analyzing emotional potential of commercials, shop windows, web designs, stationary retailing facilities). In food sciences, AFEA analyzed emotions elicited by a wide range of taste or smell stimuli and food products, including basic taste solutions [57], beverages [58], confectionary [59], and also full meals [60].

One of the advantages of analyzing facial reactions is the temporal nature of the measurement and the fact that it does not bias the subjects' natural behavior. Therefore, this methodology fits perfectly into the recent efforts to test food products in real-life situations and to investigate the effect of context on food perception and emotions with the intention to enhance external validity [60].

A general limitation is that only a few "basic" emotions are strongly associated with facial expressions, considerably fewer than used in explicit survey approaches (cf. subsection 2.1 and the number of emotions encompassed in the different scales; [34]), which potentially results in less fine-grained insights. Another disadvantage of AFEA so far is the fact, that small variations of facial expressions are not categorized into different emotions. For example, ironic or nervous grinning cannot be differentiated from a happy smile, although the emotion the underlying emotion is very different.

There are also some food-specific limitations. When emotions are measured during food consumption, oral processing including biting, chewing, and swallowing causes certain facial movements, which in turn might bias the simultaneous analysis of emotion-based facial expressions. Besides, both human coders and AFEA require high-quality video recordings of the subjects. Additionally, head movements or faces concealed by cutlery, cups, glasses, or even beards can negatively influence the quality of the results. Section 3 also demonstrates potential limitations by providing empirical examples.

EDR Electro dermal response is a measure of the electrical conductance of the skin and is widely used as a neurophysiological measure of emotional arousal. EDR is often quantified using a device called a skin conductance sensor, which consists of two electrodes that are placed on the skin (usually on the fingers or palms of the hand) to detect the electrical conductance of the skin. The sensor sends a small electric current through the skin and measures the resistance of the skin to the current. Boucsein [61] emphasizes on the multidimensionality of arousal which impedes direct interpretation of skin conductance amplitude. Complementary data collection is required to distinguish whether emotional arousal refers to the affect dimension (i.e., flight/fight) or the preparatory dimension (i.e., readiness of behavioral action). EDR is regarded as a reliable and easy-to-use instrument which does not depend on the subjects' cultural origin.

EEG Electro encephalography is a technique that measures the electrical activity of the brain. It uses electrodes placed on the scalp to detect and record the electrical impulses of neurons in the brain. These activities (amplitude and frequency of brain waves) in turn indicate different emotional states, however, special expertise is required to interpret results from such a measurement procedure. Furthermore, high-precision (and hence costly) instruments are required for exact identification of the brain region in which the neural activities take place. A more practical disadvantage might be subjects' (in particular women's) reluctance to accept electrodes on the scalp and thus potentially damage hairdressing.

PET, fMRI Positron emission tomography and functional magnetic resonance imaging are both *medical* imaging techniques. PET uses radioactive tracers, fMRI magnetic field, and radio waves to produce detailed images of the brain. For the present utilization changes in brain activity associated with different emotional states are of interest (e.g., the amygdala is known to be central for emotional processing). PET, fMRI are invasive methods and their high costs limit applications for emotion measurement.

Neural measures such as EEG, PET, and fMRI share in common that they are costly, require special expertise for executing and exploiting, are restricted to small samples and might suffer from highly controlled experimental conditions. However, they deserve credit due to the fact that they enabled the validaftion of more easy-to-use neurophysiological methods [61].

Program analyzer The program analyzer implements the concept of Mehrabian and Russell [29] that individuals approach emotionally positively but avoid emotionally negatively perceived environments (see also Rolls [10] in subsection 1.2). In more detail, subjects are exposed to certain stimuli (e.g., a commercial) and requested to move a slider toward themselves, away, respectively, and thereby continuously express emotional valence. Whereas the program analyzer was originally developed in 1937 by Lazarsfeld and Stanton to record people's moment-to-moment reactions to radio programs [62], nowadays, this audience measurement instrument has been used for testing ads (see [63]). Neibecker [64] verified reliability and validity of this procedure.

2.2.4 Observational methods using technical equipment in a real-life setting

Voice pitch analysis is a technique that involves measuring and analyzing pitch, volume, intonation, and speaking tempo of a person's voice, which can be used as an indicator of their emotional state. For example, a person's pitch may become higher when they are excited or happy, and lower when they are sad or angry. Accent or deep-throat might impede exploration. Voice pitch analysis can be done using software (e.g., PRAAT) that analyzes audio recordings of a person's voice. We note that recordings may be done in real-life (background noise might cause distortion in this case) and laboratory settings.

AFEA For automatic facial expression analysis, the setting does not make a substantial difference (and we thus refer to the previous subsection for some methodological explications). Commercial software (e.g., FaceReader provided by Noldus, EmoScan used by GfK, software provided by iMotions) and academic software (e.g., by Fraunhofer-Gesellschaft [65]) is readily available for such an analyses (see [66] for a respective overview). Technology advanced considerably such that remote analysis became feasible. Subjects in front of a laptop (or even their cellular telephone in a fixed position), and either the built-in camera or a camera mounted on the screen scans their face while viewing content.

Wearables There are several options which are available for determining the neurophysiological component of emotional arousal. Here we list those which do not require a laboratory setting. **EDR** (see subsection 2.2.3) equipment might be stored in a bag which then has to be carried by subjects when experiencing real-life settings (e.g., walking along the aisles of a supermarket). **Pupillary dilation** (the increase in the size of the pupils) can also be used as a physiological measure of emotional arousal. The size of the pupils is controlled by the sympathetic nervous system, and is known to increase during certain emotional states (such as fear, anxiety, and excitement). Pupillary dilation can be measured using infrared light (for instance as an aside when conducting mobile eye-tracking). **Heart rate** is still another physiological measure of emotional arousal. The heart rate is controlled by the autonomic nervous system, and is known to increase during certain emotional states. Heart rate can be measured in many different ways (for instance as an aside when conducting EDR). Results of both methods might be affected by other factors such as lighting / physical activity, age, and medications.

3. Examples illustrating automatic facial expressions analysis technology

The following examples aim to illustrate potential shortcomings associated with recent technological advances in facial recognition. The authors urge researchers and marketers to carefully consider raw data in line with statistical results to avoid misleading interpretations. For instance, pure emotion tracking over time (when analyzing commercials) might not necessarily yield causal relationships between the emotions expressed by the presenter and those aroused for the viewers. Besides, different measurement tools might not always result in equivalent outcomes and finally following the results without a critical reflection could lead to a wrong interpretations of the respondents' actual intentions.

3.1 Measuring emotions of a commercial

Recently, advertising and market research agencies started promoting their business portfolio by pointing to their capacity to determine the emotional impact of commercials.[2] Methods to conduct such kind of analyses differ, but frequently either the emotional appearance of the endorser (for instance a celebrity) or the emotional response of a sample of respondents (or both) are tracked continuously over the whole duration of the spot. Most commonly in such a setup, AFEA technology is employed. This example aims to demonstrate that measurements of emotions can only be viewed as an initial step because the interpretation of such data requires special competence. Some market research agencies collected data of emotional evaluations of a broad range of ads, established certain benchmarks or developed artificial intelligence-based diagnostics tools. These resources in turn enable providing management recommendations to the agencies' clients.

For this purpose,[3] we cooperated with a business (Austrian bakery Felber) and analyzed a commercial posted on social media channels (i.e., Facebook)[4] during the pandemic crisis in 2020. This bakery is a midsized company (with approximately 440 employees and about 50 shops located in Vienna[5]). In the commercial spot, the co-owner approached customers of hardware stores (as hardware stores were allowed to reopen retailing services after the first lockdown) to visit shop-in-shop outlets located in some of these hardware stores. The presenter frontally faced the camera (i.e., the audience), her face looked lighthearted, she smiled frequently and presented a variety of different products (e.g., bread, buns, bread rolls). She spoke in a dialect with the aim to target do-it-yourselfers by making use of ambiguous wording and wordplays (e.g., "You do your home yourself and Felber offers homemade bakery"). This unique and authentic presentation went viral and was heavily discussed on social media

[2] For instance, https://system1group.com/ or https://quantiface.com/

[3] We gratefully acknowledge assistance by Ms. Meyer when collecting the data.

[4] https://www.youtube.com/watch?v=I87LAyTur_k

[5] https://felberbrot.at/home.html

(while some people liked the spot very much, others disapproved her wordplay to a great extend).

Our analysis is based on three sources of information. (1) *Content of the ad.* The ad lasted about 1 min; during the first 16 s, the co-owner presented the reopening of her shops in hardware stores as a present for the upcoming Easter holidays. During the main body of the spot (seconds 17–46) she presented six different products (each for about 5 s) using humorous speech. In the last part, she essentially asked spectators to visit her stores and to purchase. (2) *Emotional expressions of the presenter.* The FaceReader (of Noldus) measured basic emotions (anger, disgust, fear, happiness, sadness, surprise) of the presenter with five observations per second. This fine-grained data pay regards to Scherer's [1], p. 702) view that "events, and particularly their appraisal, change rapidly [...] the emotional response pattering is also likely to change rapidly as a consequence." (3) *Emotional expressions of a sample of subjects.* A sample of 31 subjects watched the video and their emotions during the exposure were measured with the same granularity as indicated earlier by employing the online version of the Noldus FaceReader (data collection took place during the pandemic period which did not allow physical contacts between researchers and subjects). Data were aggregated over respondents resulting in a single trajectory for each of the six basic emotions. In order not to overload the presentation, we concentrate on the presentation of results with respect to anger and happiness which reflects the discussion about this spot in social media ([1], p. 707, also emphasizes the dominant role of these two emotions).

Figure 1 exhibits trajectories of anger and happiness aggregated over subjects and trajectories for the presenter. The horizontal axis reflexes the time shows, the three stages of the ad, and the time slots (1, ..., 6) of presenting the six products. The vertical axis is to be interpreted as intensity of measured emotions—with a domain between 0 and 1. Aggregated trajectories are much smoother because averaging balanced individual differences. In accordance with the intention of this spot, happiness is more pronounced than anger. The presenter emphasized the demonstration of her products by happy facial expressions most of the time (cf. trajectory's peaks). Subjects' happiness increased during the second part of the spot continuously but decreased during farewell. Anger does not play a role because its trajectories stayed almost constant (at a low level for all subjects, near zero for the presenter).

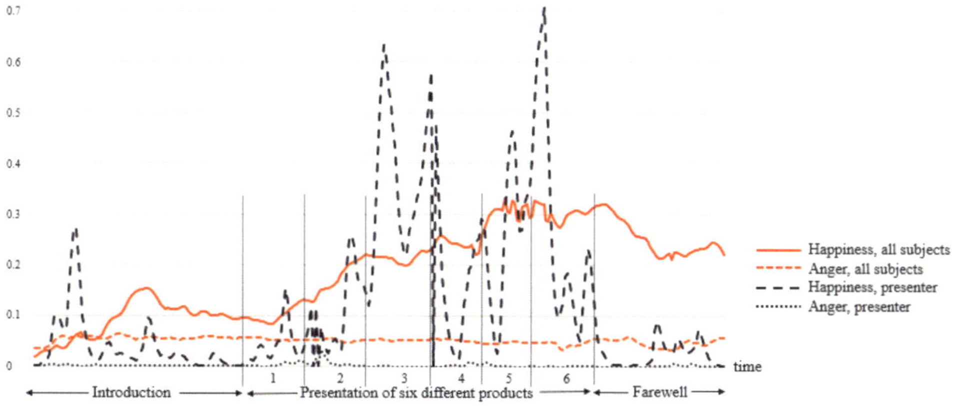

Figure 1.
Emotional trajectories during exposure to the ad.

	Anger		Happiness	
	Mean	**Standard deviation**	**Mean**	**Standard deviation**
All subjects, Y_{ti}	0.051	0.006	0.186	0.087
Presenter, X_{ti}	0.002	0.003	0.121	0.156
$Corr(X_{ti}, Y_{ti})$	−0.041		0.411	
$Corr(\Delta X_{ti}, \Delta Y_{ti})$	−0.033		0.093	

Table 2.
Descriptives of emotional trajectories for the ad.

Table 2 offers descriptive statistics for the emotional trajectories. Average values for anger are much lower than for happiness and this also applies for standard deviations. The latter is most pronounced for happiness of the presenter. Whereas these figures nicely mirror the situation depicted by **Figure 1**, we are further interested whether there is a causal relationship between the emotions expressed by the presenter and those aroused for the viewers. Or put differently, did the presenter's facial expressiveness evoke subject's emotions? From a pure data analytic standpoint, correlation coefficient might shed some light on such an echoing effect (emotional contagion). **Table 2** reports that there is no significant correlation for anger. Due to the short temporal distances between subsequent observation (five observations per second) time series of emotions (X_{ti}, Y_{ti}; t denotes time, i type of emotion) are autocorrelated and, consequently, correlation coefficients based on the raw data (X_{ti}, Y_{ti}) might be misleading. Accounting for autocorrelation, we also computed correlation coefficients based on the first differences ($\Delta X_{ti} = X_{ti} - X_{t-1\,i}$, $\Delta Y_{ti} = Y_{ti} - Y_{t-1\,i}$) which turned out to be very small (cf. **Table 2**). There might be some response latency of subjects because their reactions might not occur instantaneously. Thus, we repeated this procedure by lagging emotions from the presenter (i.e., $X_{t-s\,i}, s = 1, 2, \ldots$) but again did not find significant correlations. Consequently, inferences purely based on statistics would state that the presenter's facial expressiveness did not impact respondents' emotions (which contradicts **Figure 1** displaying increasing happiness during exposure to the ad). Of course, there might be other drivers of subjects' emotions (such as the verbal content of the presenter's presentation, her voice, the displayed products, etc.) besides her facial expressions. Nevertheless, we aim to emphasize that pure emotion tracking over time (when analyzing ads) might fall short in some aspects despite the fact that this is a powerful instrument prima facie.

3.2 Reliability of automatic facial expressions analysis

Measurement procedures based on observational methods employing a technical equipment usually score highly on aspects of reliability as potential errors due to human intervention can be prevented. The typical user of technical measurement equipment (purchased from a professional supplier) accepts the instrument provided and does not question issues of implementation. Whereas the basic idea of an AFEA (as described above) is generally accepted, implementation might vary, however. The given example highlights potential difficulties resulting therefrom, as recent literature points to the limited number of "independent peer-reviewed validation studies"

([66], p. 10). To date, prior research focuses mainly on "deliberately posed displays", as compared to naturalistic expressions.

For the present case, we compare results achieved by analyzing identical stimuli employing naturalistic expressions by two distinct, commercially available instruments (iMotions, Noldus[6]). According to their websites[7] both providers explain that the recognition software works in basically three steps: (1) the position of the face is framed within a box; (2) facial landmarks such as eyes and eye corners, brows, mouth corners, the noise tip, etc. are detected; and (3) based upon these key features classification algorithms identify action unit codes and emotional states. These algorithms make use of artificial neural networks which have been trained on large databases. These databases might vary in targeting special groups of interest (e.g., East Asians, elderly, children) and as pointed out "you might get slightly varying results when feeding the very same source material into different [classification] engines" (iMotions, p. 21).

The designs of this and the previous example have in common that short commercials (with a rather dominant endorser presenting a product or service) are used as objects of investigation, in particular, the emotional facial states of the endorsers are of interest. In this case, 13 different video clips serve as stimuli to be analyzed with AFEA (all of approximately the same length, 60 seconds). Importantly, presenters exhibit naturalistic expressions in a controlled setting. Specifically, the study employed stimuli (high-quality resolution and professional lightning) under controlled conditions by depicting full frontal shots with a neutral background and a frontal head orientation. No accessories (i.e., eyeglasses) were used to assure optimal conditions for facial recognition. The content of the commercials is not relevant in the present case, because we compare results of different measurement procedures applied to the same data. The two measurement instruments analyzed faces of these 13 presenters and provided average (calculated over the duration of the ad) amounts of emotional expressiveness for all 6 basic emotions every time: $X_{ij}^{(m)}$, with m is the type of measurement {iMotions, Noldus}, i is the type of emotion {anger, disgust, fear, happiness, sadness, surprise}, and j is the type of presentation {1, 2, ..., 13}.

Table 3 presents (selected) descriptive statistics. Focusing on presentation 1, columns 2 and 3 (rows 3–8) contrast emotional displays as measured by the two procedures (figures for both types of measurement are to be interpreted as intensity with a domain between 0 and 1). We observe considerable differences, which underpins recent findings by Dupré et al. [66], who compare eight different facial recognition tools and found that "there was considerable variance in recognition accuracy ranging from 48% to 62%" (p. 1). To emphasize this point, row 11 exhibits correlation coefficients (calculated over the type of emotion) for presenter 1. Because of the small number of observations, the nonparametric correlation coefficient due to Spearman has been included but even for this metric coherence is rather modest. Due to lack of space, **Table 3** only presents results for presentation 1 but results for the other presentations yield similar findings. The right part of **Table 3** demonstrates this claim. Rows 3–8 show correlation coefficients (calculated over presentations) for each emotion. Results are

---

[6] We chose iMotions and Noldus essentially out of convenience.

[7] https://www.academia.edu/40800374/Facial_Expression_Analysis_The_Complete_Pocket_Guide_iMotions_-Biometric_Research_Simplified_The_definitive_guide_CONTENT - iMotions https://info.noldus.com/hubfs/resources/noldus-white-paper-facereader-methodology.pdf?utm_campaign=Downloads&utm_medium=email&utm_content=59367721&utm_source=hs_automation - Noldus

	Presentation $j = 1$		$\underbrace{\text{Corr}}_{j}\left(X_{ij}^{(1)}, X_{ij}^{(2)}\right)$	
Emotions i	**Measurement iMotions**	**Measurement Noldus**	**Pearson**	**Spearman**
Anger	0.001	0.003	−0.275	−0.310
Disgust	0.095	0.111	0.064	0.474
Fear	0.060	0.093	0.690	0.508
Happiness	0.079	0.256	0.583	0.630
Sadness	0.003	0.031	0.416	0.616
Surprise	0.650	0.050	0.787	0.630
	$j = 1$		Range over j	
	Pearson	Spearman	Pearson	Spearman
$\underbrace{Corr}_{i}\left(X_{ij}^{(1)}, X_{ij}^{(2)}\right)$	−0.103	0.600	(−0.240;0.973)	(−0.131;0.941)

Table 3.
Descriptives of displayed emotions for 13 different presentations.

quite discouraging, in particular for the emotion of anger (correlations are even negative). Row 11 displays the range (over presentations) of correlation coefficients (calculated over the type of emotions). Whereas in some cases results of measurement seem to be consistent (as documented by large correlation coefficients), for others this does not seem to be the case since even negative correlations can be observed[8].

Whereas it is widely known that measurement of facial expressions might suffer from subjects' mascara, eyeglasses, knitting their eyebrows, etc. the amount of discrepancy identified in the current context is not very promising, given the claim of technology providers that the software is measuring the same phenomenon (and in the same units). We aim to explicitly emphasize that we neither favor one of the two approaches over the other nor aim to provide a recommendation at this point. Searching the relevant literature, however, we found several papers confirming validity of the Noldus software (e.g., [67]).

We definitively want to draw attention to this unfortunate state of affairs because results of investigations using AFEA technology might depend on the employed measurement approach (an unpleasant situation for a researcher). Recent studies show that "human observers clearly outperformed all automatic classifiers in recognizing emotions from both spontaneous and posed expressions" ([66], p. 11). One possible explanation for the discrepancies between human and computer-automated coding procedures as well as major differences between software providers might be ascribed to "the quality and quantity of data available to train computer-based systems [...], most current automatic classifiers have typically been trained and tested using posed or acted facial behavior" ([66], p. 11). Thus, we urge for the undertaking of clear

[8] When implementing the AFEA software several basic parameters and settings (e.g., thresholds: number of temporal frames – in which a certain pattern occurs – required in order to be considered relevant) have to be specified. We aim to point out that configurational settings were not responsible for the substantial differences identified in the given context. Standard settings were employed in both cases and demographics were specified.

efforts to consolidate these measurement procedures by considering reliability (or even validity) of this technology in a naturalistic setting.

3.3 Example from food science (self-reports vs. explicit AFEA vs. implicit AFEA)

Studying facial expressions in an implicit way might enhance the external validity of gained data, which means that such results might be better in explaining and predicting the behavior and experience of humans in real life. Therefore, a study in the test booths of the sensory Laboratory at University of Natural Resources and Life Sciences with 99 subjects compared data from an implicit face reading design with explicit data from willingly expressed facial expressions and self-reported liking. Judging products via self-reported liking by means of a 9-point hedonic scale is a widespread method in sensory science and we wanted to test whether facial expressions measured by AFEA (FaceReader 5 by Noldus Information Technology) and self-reported liking yield similar or dissimilar information.

The testing procedure in a nutshell was as follows: The subjects got instructions about the test on the notebook in front of them, but in this first phase subjects were not aware, that they were videotaped during the test. Throughout the experiment, Compusense® five (Compusense Inc.) software was used to present the questionnaire, to guide the participants through the testing procedure and for data collection. After mounting the electrodes of the autonomic nervous system measuring device on the fingers, a short familiarization phase took place, in which subjects got used to their slight pressure on the finger and generally came to rest. During the whole testing procedure subjects were video-recorded by the camera of the notebook; thus, subjects did not recognize being video-recorded. Then subjects were asked to drink a sample of juices from a shot glass (banana, orange, mixed vegetable, grapefruit, sauerkraut). A short time period after swallowing the juice was used to measure the implicit facial expressions via FaceReader. Then subjects were requested to raise their hand and to show how they liked the juice by making an appropriate face, which served as the explicit measure of their emotions. Afterwards they were also asked to rate the hedonic impression of the juice on a 9-point hedonic scale.

Highly significant differences between juice samples were detected in the implicit and in the explicit facials reactions measurements. Disgusted, happy, neutral, and sad were significant in the implicit approach and angry, disgusted, happy, neutral, and also sad in the explicit approach (**Table 4**).

Implicit facial expression	Explicit facial expression
angry	angry ***
disgusted ***	disgusted ***
happy ***	happy **
neutral ***	happy ***
sad **	sad *
scared	scared
surprised	surprised

*Note: Significant differences are marked as * ($p < 0.05$ and > 0.01), ** ($p < 0.01$ and > 0.001), *** ($p < 0.001$).*

Table 4.
Implicit and explicit facial expressions.

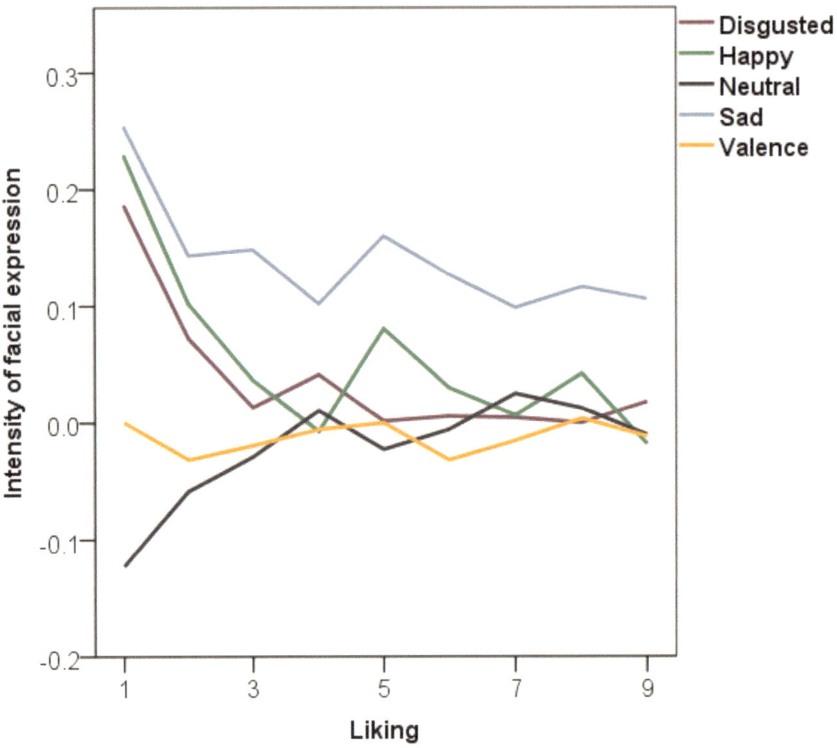

Figure 2.
Relation between self-reported liking and the intensity of emotions implicitly measured by a FaceReader.

The depiction of the coherence between explicit facial expression and self-reported liking is as expected (**Figure 2**). Disgusted and sad are highest for low liking ratings and low for high liking and vice versa is true for happy. When it comes to the relation of implicit facial expressions and self-reported liking (**Figure 3**) a remarkable aspect becomes evident. As expected, disgust and sadness are high when self-reported liking is low, but it is salient, that also happiness is high when liking is low, whereas happiness is not high for the medium to high ratings between 4 and 9 of the 9-point hedonic scale. Our hypothetical explanation is, that the FaceReader was not able to differentiate between various forms of smiling, which humans are easily able to perceive and interpret correctly as a specific, different emotions. The implicit smile subjects were showing in this study was not the expression of happiness, but it was probably a smile of rejection and embarrassment, maybe also in some cases a kind of nervous and amused laughter about the unexpected disgusting and strange sauerkraut juice we were serving to them. So, this example documents one of the limitations of an AFEA-system. Following the results of this study without critical reflection one could decide to design juice products which elicit implicit reactions detected as happy by the AFEA, which in fact do not really reflect happiness but rejection, embarrassment, ironic or nervous smile reactions to an unexpected or strange stimulus.

There is no doubt that AFEA systems are progressing quickly. New statistical methods allow better insights into the temporal development of emotions and new deep-learning algorithms have been developed to better deal with partial concealments. However, we want to draw the attention to the many shades of emotions AFEA systems are struggling with. The meaning of variants of facial expressions and the

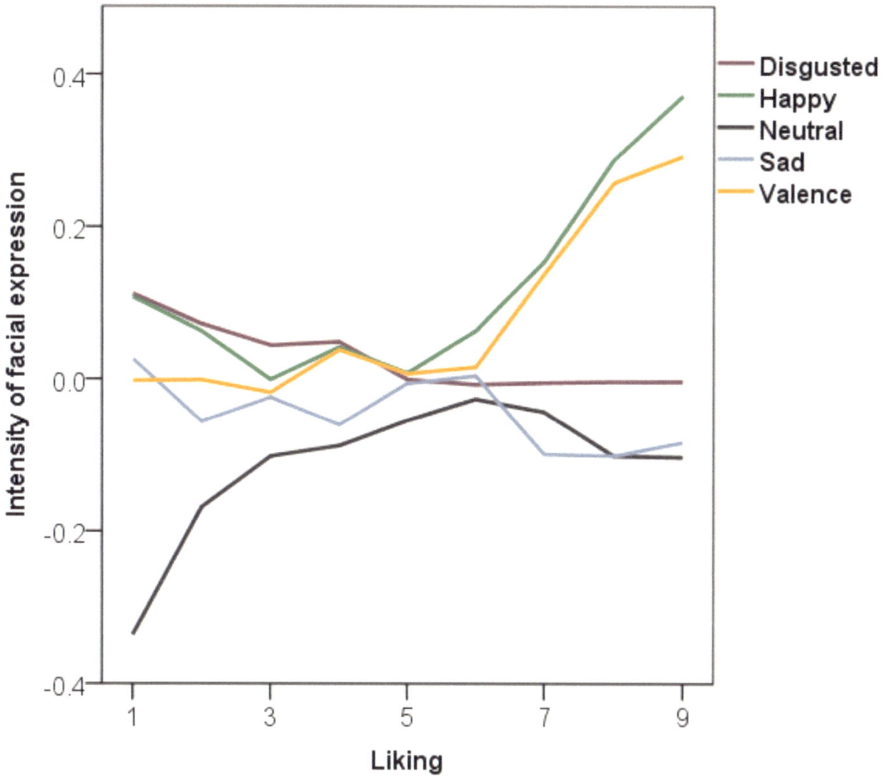

Figure 3.
Relation between self-reported liking and the intensity of willingly expressed facial emotions measured by a FaceReader.

muscle activation patterns might also be different in various cultures. Thus, without a better and more accurate and reliable categorization of facial expressions into meaningful emotions results of AFEA systems could be misleading.

4. Conclusions

This chapter provided the reader with a comprehensive overview on emotional measurements procedures. Given constrained space we limited our presentation to the basic ideas of these methods. Pointing again to Scherer's [1] component process model we emphasize that, typically, a certain method only considers one emotional component and likely falls short in accounting for others. Before deciding on a certain type of measurement, the researcher should thus determine these dimensions of the construct emotions which are of particular relevance in the current situation. Even better would be a triangulation of different methods in order to increase validity and reliability—validity of a method should never be taken for granted but always assessed in the context of the research question.

Rapid recent developments of automatic facial expressions analysis encouraged devoting special attention to AFEA. New statistical methods allow better insights in the temporal development of emotions, new algorithms have been developed to better cope with partial concealments (e.g., deep learning algorithms). Advances in software technology increased applicability, user-friendliness, processing speed and variety of results provided. Given our own experience (partly presented in Section 3), however, we again caution against the uncritical acceptance of communicated results (even from well-established research companies) but rather urge more research and efforts to increase validity and consistency of results achieved by different procedures which claim to measure the same construct when applied to identical data.

Author details

Udo Wagner[1]*, Klaus Dürrschmid[2] and Sandra Pauser[3]

1 University of Vienna and Modul University Vienna, Vienna, Austria

2 University of Natural Resources and Life Sciences (BOKU), Vienna, Austria

3 Lauder Business School, Endowed Professorship funded by the City of Vienna, Vienna, Austria

*Address all correspondence to: udo.wagner@univie.ac.at

References

[1] Scherer KR. What are emotions? And how can they be measured? Social Science Information. 2005;**44**(4): 695-729

[2] Darwin C. The Expressions of the Emotions in Man and Animals. 200th Anniversary Edition, Charles Darwin 1809–1882. London: Harper Perennial; 2009

[3] Ekman P, Rosenberg EL. What the Face Reveals: Basic and Applied Studies of Spontaneous Expression Using the Facial Action Coding System (FACS). New York: Oxford University Press; 2005

[4] Barrett LF, Adolphs R, Marsella S, Martinez AM, Pollak SD. Emotional expressions reconsidered: Challenges to inferring emotion from human facial movements. Psychological Science in the Public Interest. 2019;**20**(1):1-68

[5] Mesquita B. Emotions in collectivist and individualist contexts. Journal of Personality and Social Psychology. 2001; **80**(1):68-74

[6] Frijda NH. Emotions and hedonic experience. In: Kahneman D, Diener E, Schwarz N, editors. Well-being: Foundations of Hedonic Psychology. New York, NY: Russell Sage Foundation; 1999. pp. 190-210

[7] Frijda NH. The Emotions. Cambridge: Cambridge University Press; 1986

[8] Izard CE. Four systems for emotion activation: Cognitive and noncognitive processes. Psychological Review. 1993; **100**:68-90

[9] Oatley K, Johnson-Laird PN. Towards a cognitive theory of emotions. Cognition and Emotion. 1987;**1**(1):29-50

[10] Rolls ET. Emotion Explained. Affective Science. New York: Oxford University Press; 2005

[11] Gibson EL. Emotional influences on food choice: sensory, physiological and psychological pathways. Physiology & Behavior. 2006;**89**:53-61

[12] Oatley K, Johnson-Laird PN. Cognitive approaches to emotions. Trends in Cognitive Sciences. 2014; **18**(3):134-140

[13] Frijda NH, Parrott WG. Basic emotions or ur-emotions? Emotion Review. 2011;**3**(4):406-415

[14] Russell JA. Core affect and the psychological construction of emotion. Psychological Review. 2003;**110**(1):145-172

[15] Clore GL. Why emotions are never unconscious. In: The Nature of Emotion: Fundamental Questions. 1994. pp. 285-290

[16] Winkielman P, Berridge K, Sher S. Emotion, consciousness, and social behavior. In: Decety J, Cacioppo JT, editors, Handbook of Social Neuroscience. New York, NY: Oxford University Press; 2011. pp. 195-211

[17] James W. What is emotion? Mind. 1884;**9**(34):188-205

[18] Lange CG. Om sindsbevaegelser; et psyko-fysiologisk studie. In Deutsch 1887: Ueber Gemüthsbe-Wegungen: Eine Psycho-Physiologische Studie. Kopenhagen: Jacob Lunds Forlag; 1885

[19] Damasio A. Descartes' Error. Emotion, Reason and the Human Brain. New York, NY: Random House; 2006

[20] Danner L, Duerrschmid K. Chapter 10: Automatic facial expressions analysis in consumer science. In: Ares G,

Varela P, editors. Methods in Consumer Research. Vol. 2. Sawston: Woodhead Publishing; 2018. pp. 231-252

[21] Danner L, Dürrschmid K. Automatic facial expressions analysis in consumer science. In: Methods in Consumer Research. Vol. 2. London: Elsevier Ltd.; 2018. pp. 231-252

[22] Coppin G, Sander D. Theoretical approaches to emotion and its measurement. In: Meiselman HL, editor. Emotion Measurement, 2nd edition. Duxford, UK: Woodhead Publishing; 2021. pp. 3-37

[23] De Houwer J, Moors A. How to define and examine the implicitness of implicit measures. In: Proctor R, Capaldi J, editors. Implicit Measures of Attitudes. New York, NY: The Guilford Press; 2007. pp. 179-194

[24] Dijksterhuis G. Implicit Methods' Merits. A Sense of Diversity, Second European Conference on Sensory and Consumer Scuience of Food and Beverages. The Hague, Netherlands: Elsevier Ltd.; 2006

[25] Zarantonello L, Luomala HT. Dear Mr Chocolate: Constructing a typology of contextualized chocolate consumption experiences through qualitative diary research. Qualitative Market Research: An International Journal. 2011;**14**(1):55-82

[26] Kirchler E, De Rosa AS. Wirkungsanalyse von Werbebotschaften mittels Assoziationsgeflecht. Spontane Reaktionen auf und überlegte Beschreibung von Benetton-Werbebildern. Jahrbuch der Absatz-und Verbrauchsforschung. 1996;**42**:67-89

[27] Zaltman G, Coulter RH. Seeing the voice of the customer: Metaphor-based advertising research. Journal of Advertising Research. 1995;**35**(4):35-51

[28] Izard CE. Human Emotions. New York: Plenum; 1977

[29] Mehrabian A, Russel JA. An Approch to Environment Psychology. Cambridge: MIT Press; 1974

[30] Plutchik R. A general psychoevolutionary theory of emotion. In: Plutchik R, Kellerman H, editors. Theories of Emotion. Academic Press; 1980. pp. 3-33

[31] Watson D, Clark LA, Tellegen A. Development and validation of brief measures of positive and negative affect: The PANAS scales. Journal of Personality and Social Psychology. 1988;**54**(6): 1063-1070

[32] Richins ML. Measuring emotions in the consumption experience. Journal of Consumer Research. 1997;**24**(2):127-146

[33] Jager G, Schlich P, Tijssen I, Yao J, Visalli M, de Graaf C, et al. Temporal dominance of emotions: Measuring dynamics of food-related emotions during consumption. Food Quality and Preference. 2014;**37**:87-99

[34] King SC, Meiselman HL. Development of a method to measure consumer emotions associated with foods. Food Quality and Preference. 2010;**21**(2):168-177

[35] Nestrud MA, Meiselman HL, King SC, Lesher LL, Cardello AV. Development of EsSense25, a shorter version of the EsSense Profile®. Food Quality and Preference. 2016;**48**(A):107-117

[36] Cardello AV, Jaeger SR. Questionnaires should be the default method in food-related emotion research. Food Quality and Preference. 2021;**92**:104180

[37] Lang PJ. Behavioral treatment and biobehavioral assessment: Computer

applications. In: Sidowski JB, Johnson JH, Williams TA, editors. Technology in Mental Health Delivery. Norwood, NJ: Ablex; 1980. pp. 119-137

[38] Desmet PMA, Hekkert P, Jacobs JJ. When a car makes you smile: Development and application of an instrument to measure product emotions. Advances in Consumer Research. 2000;**27**(1):111-117

[39] Gutjar S, de Graaf C, Kooijman V, de Wijk RA, Nys A, ter Horst GJ, et al. The role of emotions in food choice and liking. Food Research International. 2015;**76**:216-223

[40] Groeppel-Klein A, Hupp O, Broeckelmann P, Dieckmann A. Measurement of emotions elicited by advertising. ACR North American Advances. 2010;**37**:497-498

[41] Vermeer F. Snijbloemen versterken positieve gevoelens en stemmingen: Wetenschappelijk onderzoek naar het effect van snijbloemen op de gemoedstoestand van de mens. Zoetermeer: Intern rapport Productschap Tuinbouw Nederland; 2009

[42] Mojet J, Dürrschmid K, Danner L, Jöchl M, Heiniö RL, Holthuysen N, et al. Are implicit emotion measurements evoked by food unrelated to liking? Food Research International. 2015;**76**(P2): 224-232

[43] Greenwald AG, McGhee DE, Schwartz JLK. Measuring individual differences in implicit cognition: The implicit association test. Journal of Personality and Social Psychology. 1998; **74**:1464-1480

[44] Burgoon JK, Hoobler G. Nonverbal signals. In: Knapp ML, Daly J, editors. Handbook of Interpersonal Communication. Thousand Oaks, CA: Sage; 2002. pp. 240-299

[45] Ekman P. Emotions revealed. BMJ. 2004;**328**(Suppl. S5):0405184

[46] Hwang HC, Matsumoto D. 6: Measuring emotions in the face. In: Meiselman HL, editor. Emotion Measurement. Amsterdam: Woodhead Publishing; 2016. pp. 125-144

[47] Wagner HL. Methods for the study of facial behavior. In: Russell JA, Fernández-Dols JM, editors. The Psychology of Facial Expression. Cambridge: Cambridge University Press; 1997. pp. 31-54

[48] Ekman P, Friesen WV. Facial Action Coding System. Environmental Psychology & Nonverbal Behavior. Palo Alto, CA: Consulting Psychologists Press; 1978

[49] Zeinstra GG, Koelen MA, Colindres D, Kok FJ, de Graaf C. Facial expressions in school-aged children are a good indicator of 'dislikes', but not of 'likes'. Food Quality and Preference. 2009;**20**(8):620-624

[50] Le Goff G, Delarue J. Non-verbal evaluation of acceptance of insect-based products using a simple and holistic analysis of facial expressions. Food Quality and Preference. 2017;**56**:285-293

[51] Frey S, Hirsbrunner HP, Pool J, Daw W. Das Berner System zur Untersuchung nonverbaler Interaktion: I. Die Erhebung des Rohdatenprotokolls. In: Winkler P, editor. Methoden der Analyse von face-to-face Situationen. Stuttgart: Metzlersche Verlagsbuchhandlung; 1981. pp. 203-236

[52] Weinberg P. Nonverbale Marktkommunikation. Heidelberg: Springer; 2013

[53] Wang EST, Tsai BK, Chen TL, Chang SC. The influence of emotions displayed and personal selling on customer behaviour intention. The Service Industries Journal. 2012;**32**(3): 353-366

[54] Hu S, Player KA, McChesney KA, Dalistan MD, Tyner CA, Scozzafava JE. Facial EMG as an indicator of palatability in humans. Physiology & Behavior. 1999;**68**(1):31-35

[55] Sato W, Minemoto K, Ikegami A, Nakauma M, Funami T, Fushiki T. Facial EMG correlates of subjective hedonic responses during food consumption. Nutrients. 2020;**12**(4):1174

[56] Sato W, Yoshikawa S, Fushiki T. Facial EMG activity is associated with hedonic experiences but not nutritional values while viewing food images. Nutrients. 2020;**13**(1):11-24

[57] Zhi R, Cao L, Cao G. Asians' facial responsiveness to basic tastes by automated facial expression analysis system. Journal of Food Science. 2017; **82**(3):794-806

[58] Mehta A, Sharma C, Kanala M, Thakur M, Harrison R, Torrico DD. Self-reported emotions and facial expressions on consumer acceptability: A study using energy drinks. Food. 2021;**10**(2):330-346

[59] Gunaratne TM, Fuentes S, Gunaratne NM, Torrico DD, Gonzalez Viejo C, Dunshea FR. Physiological responses to basic tastes for sensory evaluation of chocolate using biometric techniques. Food. 2019; **8**(7):243

[60] De Wijk RA, Kaneko D, Dijksterhuis GB, van Zoggel M, Schiona I, Visalli M, et al. Food perception and emotion measured over time in-lab and in-home. Food Quality and Preference. 2019;**75**: 170-178

[61] Boucsein W. Electrodermal Activity. New York: Springer Science & Business Media; 2012

[62] Levy M. The Lazarsfeld-Stanton program analyser: An historical note. Journal of Communication. 2006;**32**(4): 30-38

[63] Wagner U, Ebster C, Eberhardsteiner L, Prenner M. The after-effects of fear-inducing public service announcements. In: Dawid H, Doerner K, Feichtinger G, Kort P, Seidl A, editors. Dynamic Perspectives on Managerial Decision Making. Dynamic Modeling and Econometrics in Economics and Finance. Heidelberg: Springer; 2016. pp. 395-411

[64] Neibecker B. Konsumentenemotionen Messung durch computergestützte Verfahren: Eine empirische Validierung nicht-verbaler Methoden. Würzburg: Springer; 1985

[65] Ploger AOP, Valdenegro-Toro M. Image captioning of classification of dangerous situations, working paper. 2017. Available from: https://arxiv.org/abs/1711.02578.

[66] Dupré D, Krumhuber EG, Küster D, McKeown GJ. A performance comparison of eight commercially available automatic classifiers for facial affect recognition. PLoS One. 2020; **15**(4):1-17

[67] Skiendziel T, Rösch AG, Schultheiss OC. Assessing the convergent validity between the automated emotion recognition software Noldus FaceReader 7 and Facial Action Coding System Scoring. PLoS One. 2019; **14**(10):e0223905

Chapter 7

Feature Extraction for Emotion Recognition: A Review

Neha Garg and Kamlesh Sharma

Abstract

With the increasing role of Artificial Intelligence and ubiquitous computing paradigms, a stage has arrived where human being and machine is interacting seamlessly. However, the users may face issues while interacting with these systems. A more simple and reliable interaction with machines will be possible by recognizing user's emotions. In order to develop a system that can respond effectively to user's emotions can be modeled by utilizing the electroencephalogram (EEG) as a bio-signal sensor. The emotion recognition plays a vital role in the area of Human Computer Interaction (HCI) and Brain Computer Interaction (BCI) to provide good interaction between brain and machine. The emotion recognition comprises of three major phases feature extraction, feature selection and classifiers. The present chapter provides an overview of feature extraction techniques utilized by researchers in frequency domain analysis, time domain analysis and time-frequency domain analysis. The chapter also discusses the process, issues and challenges for feature extraction in EEG, the application area of the EEG.

Keywords: emotion recognition (ER), human computer interaction (HCI), brain computer interaction (BCI), feature extraction, electroencephalogram (EEG)

1. Introduction

The world in the verge of paradigm change in the field of Intelligent Systems: moving from an era in which people control gadgets to one in which autonomous devices, capable of self-management and aware of their environmental and situational context [1]. As per the definition of Ubiquitous Computing conceived by Mark Weiser [2], the world is approaching to a level of automation and computing where human and computers are interacting with each other naturally without the awareness of users. Ironically, one of the major issue is growing complexity with this paradigm shift is that user find it difficult to interact with such systems [3]. As a result, it's crucial to identify all potential interaction modalities and organize them according to problem domain. For example personalized interaction is highly required in computer- mediated interaction like virtual reality to maintain user's interest and engagement with the cognitive activity. Task engagement includes both the user's cognitive activity and engagement but it also requires an understanding of user's emotional transfer. Therefore, the physiological computing system can be used to provide insights into the cognitive and emotional processes involved in completing tasks [4]. In particular, the display of level of brain activity by processing EEG signals may be of benefits when integrated with input modality [5]. ER can be performed with the help of physiological and non-physiological signals [6].

Facial expressions, speech, voice, actions etc., are the non-physiological signals that could not contribute very precisely for ER [7]. EEG signals have proved strong implications in finding emotions states [8]. The classification accuracy for emotion recognition is higher for EEG signals and the model can also the changes in mood too [9].

2. Broad area description

With the advancement of technology HCI is providing the support to BCI. Providing machines with the capacity to understand and discover the various emotional states of users can be of essential significance for the next generation. Endowing digital devices with logical reasoning abilities about user affective context will provide the facility to detect the present state of feelings. Such as signs of feeling low, frustrated, fear and allow the machine to react in a more intellectual and empathetic way [10]. As a result, this collectively along with other HCI traits like consistency, flexibility, and usability may give the base to produce more clever and more adaptive interface [11]. Now a day's various input modalities have been utilized to gather the input data for emotion recognition. The very first of them is audiovisual based communication along with eye gazed, facial expression, speech evaluation, etc. The second physiological measure is sensor based signals along with EEG signals; galvanic skin response and electrocardiogram can also be used [12].

3. What is emotion?

The emotion can be the affective aspect of consciousness or mental reaction or can be states a strong feeling towards a particular object and it can have some associated physiological and behavioral changes in voice, expression or mood, etc. The signals of emotions can be categorized into two categories physiological signals and non-physiological signals [13].

The physiological reactions can be the increment or decrement the value of EEG signals, body temperature, heartbeats, blood pressure, breathing rate, etc. the studies states the more impact of physiological reactions on women in comparison with the men [13]. The non-physiological reactions include the expressions, action, voice etc. Here physiological signals are difficult to ignore during data acquisition stage and provides more accurate result [14].

The researchers have proposed various emotion models based on discrete model and dimension model theory [6]. The theory proposed by P. Ekman has six primary emotional states surprise, happiness, fear, anger, disgust, and sadness [15]. The other complex emotions are secondary one that is the composition of these basic emotions. P. Lang proposed a dimensional model called valence- arousal model [16]. The model maps emotions into two-dimensional space where valence represents positive and negative conditions and arousal represents the intensity of human emotions. This model maps different emotions at same place, which results in difficulty to distinguish. The model has been represented in **Figure 1**. To overcome this issue, A. Mehrabian has proposed model by adding dominance dimension to the valence-arousal model [18]. This model is called Pleasure-Arousal-Dominance (PAD) model.

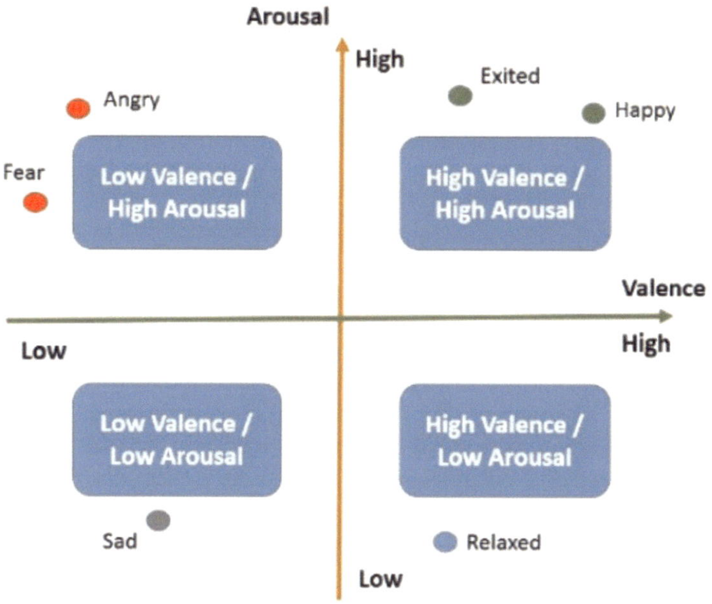

Figure 1.
Arousal valence based emotion model [17].

4. Characteristics of EEG signals

The EEG different frequency bands are related to conscious human activities [19]. Based on the frequency of EEG signals, the signals are divided into five categories, alpha, beta, gamma, theta and delta.

Delta signal has frequency of range 0.5–4 Hz and occurs in the state of unconsciousness such as dreamless, deep sleep. Theta signals occur with frequency of 4–8 Hz and appear in the state of sub consciousness like sleepiness, dreaming etc. Alpha waves arise at frequency 8–13 Hz frequency when in consciousness human is in relaxed state. Alpha waves have higher oscillatory energy in neutral and negative emotions than beta and gamma waves.

Beta waves occur when human mind is highly concentrated and active with frequency 13–30 Hz. The active state of mind can be dictated by taking average power ratio of beta and alpha waves. Gamma waves occur at very high frequency greater than 30 Hz and show the hyperactivity of brain. As the results suggest, that emotional EEG is more evoked in lower frequency band in comparison to higher frequency band. Similarly negative emotions have higher intensity and wider distribution than positive ones [20].

5. Features of EEG signals

EEG signal is a weak physiological signal, which is highly utilized by researchers for emotion recognition due to the high accuracy of results [6]. For emotion recognition, the features of EEG signals categorized in categories spatial domain features, time domain features, frequency domain features and time-frequency domain features.

5.1 Spatial domain features

Spatial analysis is distribution of electrical signals at different regions of mind during acquisition of EEG signals. Different regions of brain respond in a different manner to emotions [21], considering how spectral, spatial and temporal aspects complement each other. To consider both spatial-temporal and spatial-spectral characteristics parallel streams are created.

5.2 Time domain features

EEG signals are often recorded in the form of time domain which is statistical in nature. Time domain analysis is commonly performed by using histogram analysis or statistical methods [6]. However the time-domain features include EEG signals with less information loss. But due to complex form of EEG signals, there is no standard unified method for analysis. So the analysts need to be rich in knowledge and experience.

5.3 Frequency domain features

Frequency domain features are obtained after converting the original time domain signal using Fourier Transformation. The aim of frequency domain is to find the frequency information of signals along with power characteristics of various frequency bands.

5.4 Time-frequency domain features

The time-domain and frequency domain signals are merged to examine EEG signals more accurately. As convergence process of signals from time domain to frequency domain does not lost the time information.

Time- frequency analysis has the ability to completely reflect the distinctive information in EEG signals. Continuous wavelet transforms (CWT) and discrete wavelet transform (DWT) are the two primary forms of wavelet transformation, which separate the low-frequency component of the signals. It is more advantageous than the conventional approaches for dealing nonlinear and non-stationary signals.

6. Methodology

The Emotion Recognition using EEG signals process is comprises of four phases as shown in **Figure 2**.

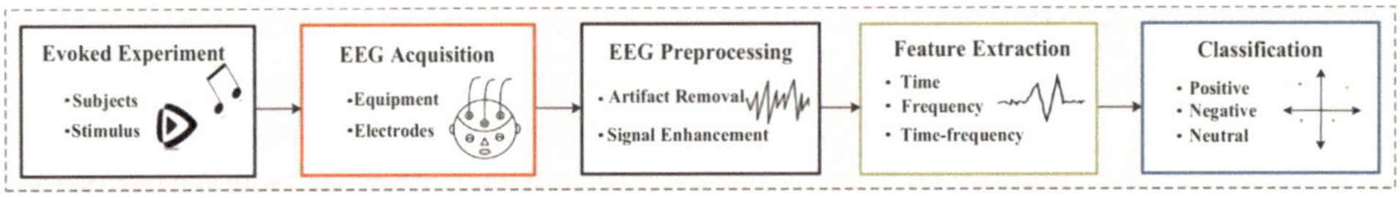

Figure 2.
Emotion classification process for EEG signals [6].

1. EEG Signal Acquisition—The collection of EEG signals can be divided into two methods—invasive and non-invasive. Here, the data collected using invasive method has higher signal to noise ration while non-invasive has utilization in BCI. The collection of EEG signals can be divided into two methods- invasive and non-invasive. Here, the data collected using invasive method has higher signal to noise ration while non-invasive has utilization in BCI. The first part comprises of four ways to collect EEG signals [22]; the first technique is electroencephalogram i.e. is graph obtained by recording and amplifying the brain's signals. The signals are collected with the help of electrodes which are fixed in scalp. The second method is Electrocorticogram (ECoG). In ECoG, the recording is performed by surgically implanted electrodes. ECoG provides better spatial resolution and accuracy. Another method of signal acquisition is Functional Magnetic Resonance Imaging (fMRI), is a neuroimaging technique. fMRI reflect the oxygen saturation and blood flow level through the measurement of MR signals. Depth electrode is the fourth method of EEG signal detection. Deep Brain Simulation (DBS) is performed by placing electrodes at specific regions of brain to deliver current.

2. Pre-processing—the pre-processing phase comprises of removal of artifacts, thresholding of the output, amplifying the signals, edge detection and signal averaging etc. [23].

3. Feature Extraction—the feature selection phase is used to find a feature vector. Here, feature denotes a distinctive or characteristic measurement from a segment of pattern which plays a useful part in classification. For linear analysis of one-dimensional signals for either frequency or time domain, the various method has been discussed below:

a. Fast Fourier Transformation (FFT) method

The fast Fourier Transformation (FFT) is a simple and fast way of Discrete Fourier Transformation (DFT). FFT utilized to filter signals from the time domain to the frequency domain. FET is good for stationary signals. However the overall EEG signals are not stationary in nature but for particular band it can be utilized.

Welch's method is one of the methods for transforming EEG signals using Fourier transformation [24]. The data sequencing is applied to data windowing, where data sequence x_i (n) and Fourier transformation is represented as

$$x_i(n) = \left(\frac{1}{L}\right)\sum_{k=1}^{L} X(k)\omega_L{}^{-(n-1)(k-1)} \tag{1}$$

$$X(k) = \sum_{n=1}^{L} x(n)\omega_L{}^{(n-1)(k-1)} \tag{2}$$

b. Wavelet Transformation (WT) method

WT plays a vital role in the field of diagnostic and recognition, which compresses the time-varying signal, into few parameters that represents the nature of signal [25]. The model uses time-frequency domain with a variable size windows to provide more flexibility to the systems. WT can be categorized in two ways continuous WT and discrete WT.

c. Eigenvectors

The eigenvector methods are utilized to calculate signals frequency and power from artifact ruled measurements. The essence of the techniques is to correlate the corrupted signals using Eigen decomposition [26]. The techniques that employed eigenvector are MUSIC method, Pisarenko's method and minimum norm method.

d. Time-frequency distribution

The Time-frequency domain is utilized with the stationary and noiseless signal, that's why windowing process is required for pre-processing. The various methods are used for TFD model like Short-time Fourier Transform (STFT), wavelet packet transformation (WPT) and Hilbert-Huang transformation (HHT).

e. Autoregressive method

Autoregressive (AR) method is advantageous for short data segment analysis. It also limits the loss of spectral leakage and provides better frequency resolution. Yule-Walker method and Burg's method are used in AR model for spectral estimation.

Method name	**Advantages**	**Disadvantages**	**Analysis method**	**Suitability**
Fast Fourier transform	i. Good tool for stationary signal processing ii. It is more appropriate for narrowband signal, such as sine wave iii. It has an enhanced speed over virtually all other available methods in real-time applications	i. Weakness in analyzing nonstationary signals such as EEG ii. It does not have good spectral estimation and cannot be employed for analysis of short EEG signals iii. FFT cannot reveal the localized spikes and complexes that are typical among epileptic seizures in EEG signals iv. FFT suffers from large noise sensitivity, and it does not have shorter duration data record	Frequency domain	Narrowband, stationary signals
Wavelet transform	i. It has a varying window size, being broad at low	Needs selecting a proper mother wavelet	Both time and freq.	Transient and stationary signal

Method name	Advantages	Disadvantages	Analysis method	Suitability
	frequencies and narrow at high frequencies ii. It is better suited for analysis of sudden and transient signal changes iii. Better poised to analyze irregular data patterns, that is, impulses existing at different time instances		domain, and linear	
Eigenvector	Provides suitable resolution to evaluate the sinusoid from the data	Lowest eigenvalue may generate false zeros when Pisarenko's method is employed	Frequency domain	Signal buried with noise
Time frequency distribution	i. It gives the feasibility of examining great continuous segments of EEG signal ii. TFD only analyses clean signal for good results	i. The time-frequency methods are oriented to deal with the concept of stationary; as a result, windowing process is needed in the preprocessing module ii. It is quite slow (because of the gradient ascent computation) iii. Extracted features can be dependent on each other	Both time and frequency domains	Stationary signal
Autoregressive	i. AR limits the loss of spectral problems and yields improved frequency resolution ii. Gives good frequency resolution iii. Spectral analysis based on AR model is particularly advantageous when short data segments are analyzed, since the frequency resolution of an analytically derived AR spectrum is infinite and does not depend on the length of analyzed data	i. The model order in AR spectral estimation is difficult to select ii. AR method will give poor spectral estimation once the estimated model is not appropriate, and model's orders are incorrectly selected iii. It is readily susceptible to heavy biases and even large variability	Frequency domain	Signal with sharp spectral features

Table 1.
Comparison of various feature extraction techniques [26].

Method	Frequency resolution	Spectral leakage
FFT	LOW	HIGH
WT	HIGH	LOW
AR	HIGH	LOW

Table 2.
Comparison of frequency resolution and spectral leakage of feature extraction techniques [27].

The comparison of various models along with their advantages and disadvantages has been tabulated below in **Table 1**.

As we have discussed, the various techniques for feature extraction of EEG signals, **Table 2** representing a comparative analysis for frequency resolution and spectral leakage from where one can easily conclude that AR method is utilized where one need to avoid spurious features.

4. Classification- the final stage of EEG signals processing is classification. Machine learning classifiers are hugely deployed to use features to predict the corresponding class. The classification is performed in three categories: positive, neutral and negative [28]. Algorithms like Support Vector Machine (SVM), Naive Bayes (NB), Random Forest (RF), etc. Are hugely used by researchers due to their simplicity and accuracy [6]. But these techniques never consider the temporal information associated with EEG signals.

Recently deep learning algorithms like Convolution Neural Network (CNN), Recurrent Neural Network (RNN), Artificial Neural Network (ANN), etc. are also applied by researchers for relatively high accuracy [29].

7. Applications of EEG signals

Few application of emotion detection using EEG signals has been discussed below:

1. Medical diagnosis—the signals collected using EEG can be used to diagnose various diseases related to brain like brain edema, Parkinson's disease, epilepsy scots, etc.

2. Education—studies has shown that there are some emotional states that are helpful for learning [17]. So by given different educational task and acquire signal during them can help in studying the impact on human.

3. Video gaming—video games are to entertain player and making them attached and involved [30]. By analyzing the mood and mind-set of users, the video games can engage users emotionally, which may result in good participation rate.

The application are not restricted to these three categories only, they are also applicable in Brain Computer Interaction (BCI), Patient Care, Driving Autonomous Car, etc.

8. Solutions and recommendations

In this chapter, we have presented different machine learning algorithm and techniques and their comparison that are used for emotion recognition. In emotion recognition there is no direct approach that suite for all kind of applications. There are multiple factors that affect the choice of machine learning algorithm. The usefulness of emotion recognition and its application has been discussed. Machine algorithms are used to analyze data used for classification. The algorithm basically filter data into categories, which is achieved by providing a set of training examples, each set marked as belonging to one or the other of the two categories.

9. Future scope and conclusion

The future of emotion recognition is very bright. Emotion recognition is already an incredibly powerful tool that helps to solve really hard classification of emotions problems. With the use of emotion recognition, a very hard problem can be solved and system can be work as per the mood and feelings of users.

Author details

Neha Garg* and Kamlesh Sharma
Faculty of Engineering and Technology, Computer Science and Engineering, Manav Rachna International Institute of Research and Studies, Faridabad, Haryana, India

*Address all correspondence to: gargsneha99@gmail.com

References

[1] Ark WS. A systematic approach to occupancy modelling in ambient sensor-rich buildings. IBM Systems Journal. 1999;**38**(4):504-507

[2] Weiser M. The computer for the 21st century. Scientific American. 1991;**256**: 94-104

[3] Pantic M, Nijholt A, Pentland A, Huanag TS. Humancentred intelligent human-computer interaction (hci): How far are we from attaining it? International Journal of Autonomous and Adaptive Communications Systems. 2008;**1**(2):168-187

[4] Fairclough SH, Gilleade K, Ewing KC, Roberts J. Capturing user engagement via psychophysiology: Measures and mechanisms for biocybernetic adaptation. International Journal of Autonomous and Adaptive Communications Systems. 2013;**6**(1): 63-79. DOI: 10.1504/IJAACS.2013.050694

[5] Szafir D, Mutlu B. Pay attention!: Designing adaptive agents that monitor and improve user engagement. In: Proceedings of the SIGCHI Conference on Human Factors in Computing Systems. New York, NY, USA: ACM; 2012. pp. 11-20. DOI: 10.1145/2207676.2207679

[6] Wang J, Wang M. Review of the emotional feature extraction and classification using EEG signals. Cognitive Robotics. 2021;**1**: 29-40

[7] Zhang T, Zheng W, Cui Z, Zong Y, Yan J, Yan K. A deep neural network-driven feature learning method for multi-view facial expression recognition. IEEE Transactions on Multimedia. 2016; **18**(12):2528-2536

[8] Zheng WL, Lu BL. Investigating critical frequency bands and channels for eeg-based emotion recognition with deep neural networks. IEEE Transactions on Autonomics Mental Diseaases. 2015; **7**(3):162-175

[9] Hilborn O. Evaluating classifiers for emotion recognition using EEG. Lecture Notes in Computer Science. 2015;**8027**: 492-501

[10] Picard RW. Affective computing: Challenges. International Journal of Human-Computer Studies. 2003;**59**(1): 55-64

[11] Dix A, Finlay J, Abowd GD, Beale R. Human-computer Interaction. 2004. Available from: http://www.amazon.com/Human-Computer-Interaction3rd-Alan-Dix/dp/0130461091

[12] Burle B, Spieser L, Roger C, Casini L, Hasbroucq T, Vidal F. Spatial and temporal resolutions of eeg: Is it really black and white? A scalp current density view. International Journal of Psychophysiology. 2015;**97**(3):210-220. on the benefits of using surface Laplacian (current source density) methodology in electrophysiology. [Online]. Available from: http://www.sciencedirect.com/science/article/pii/S016787601500186

[13] Cao KX. The Research of the EEG Frequency Power Feature in Three Basic Emotions. Tianjin, China: Tianjin Medical University; 2019

[14] Fathalla RS, Alshehri WS. Emotions recognition and signal classification: A state-of-the-art. International Journal of Synthetic Emotions (IJSE). 2020;**11**(1):1-16

[15] Ekman P. An argument for basic emotions. Cognition & Emotion. 1992;**6** (3–4):169-200

[16] Lang PJ. The emotion probe: Studies of motivation and attention. American Psychologist. 1995;**50**(5):372

[17] Kołakowska A, Landowska A, Szwoch M, Szwoch W, Wróbel MR. Emotion recognition and its application in software engineering. In: 2013 6th International Conference on Human System Interactions (HSI). Vol. 10. IEEE; 2013. pp. 532-539

[18] Mehrabian A. Comparison of the PAD and PANAS as models for describing emotions and for differentiating anxiety from depression. Journal of Psychopathology Behavioral Assessment. 1997;**19**(4):331-357

[19] Liu Z, Xie Q, Wu M, Cao W, Li D, Li S. Electroencephalogram emotion recognition based on empirical mode decomposition and optimal feature selection. IEEE Transactions Cognition Developmental System. 2019;**11**(4): 517-526

[20] Zhang JX, Bo H. Research on EEG emotion recognition based on CNN. Modified Computer. 2018;**8**: 12-16

[21] Jia Z, Lin Y, Cai X. SST-EmotionNet: Spatial-spectral-temporal based attention 3D dense network for EEG emotion recognition MM '20. In: The 28th ACM International Conference on Multimedia. ACM; 2020. pp. 2909-2917

[22] Li B, Cheng T, Guo Z. A review of EEG acquisition, processing and application. Journal of Physics: Conference Series. 2021;**1907**(1):012045

[23] Garg N, Sharma K. Text preprocessing for sentiment analysis based on social network data. International Journal of Electrical and Computer Engineering (IJECE). 2022; **12**(1):776-784

[24] Faust O, Acharya RU, Allen AR, Lin CM. Analysis of EEG signals during epileptic and alcoholic states using AR modeling techniques. IRBM. 2008;**29**(1): 44-52

[25] Cvetkovic D, Übeyli ED, Cosic I. Wavelet transform feature extraction from human PPG, ECG, and EEG signal responses to ELF PEMF exposures: A pilot study. Digital Signal Processing. 2008;**18**(5):861-874

[26] Al-Fahoum AS, Al-Fraihat AA. Methods of EEG signal features extraction using linear analysis in frequency and time-frequency domains. International Scholarly Research Notices. 2014

[27] Agarwal R, Gotman J, Flanagan D, Rosenblatt B. Automatic EEG analysis during long-term monitoring in the ICU. Electroencephalography and Clinical Neurophysiology. 1998;**107**(1):44-58

[28] Garg N, Sharma K. Annotated Corpus creation for sentiment analysis in code-mixed Hindi-English (Hinglish) social network data. Indian Journal of Science and Technology. 2020;**13**(40): 4216-4224

[29] Chen D-W et al. A feature extraction method based on differential entropy and linear discriminant analysis for emotion recognition. Sensors. 2019; **19**(7):1631

[30] Adams E. Fundamentals of Game Design. Pearson Education; 2009